God, Are You Listening? I Need Help! is the cry of every anguished heart facing life's problems. Using the words of Scripture and biblical stories of God's protective care, Pastor Jo shows us how He is always working with us for our good in every situation. Her practical examples reach us right where we are, no matter how hopeless we may feel. I know this book will speak encouragement to anyone who feels lost and alone in today's hectic world as well as in generations to come. He *is* listening!

—Pastor Larry Reece
Cape Henry Church, Virginia Beach, VA

This book instructs followers of Jesus on how to get a breakthrough in their walk with God. The author, Pastor JoAnne Ramsay, begins with the importance of forgiveness, reminding us that if we want to be like Christ, we must forgive like Him. *God, Are You Listening? I Need Help! i*s an anointed book of biblical revelation that can revolutionize your thinking and your prayers!

—Dr. Travis Thigpen, Apostle
Gateway Ministries, Richmond, VA

Pastor Jo is an anointed speaker who brings life to God's Word through her dynamic style of teaching and writing. Her knowledge of Scripture and her application of the Word inspires the Body of Christ through her radio broadcasts, YouTube videos, and personal appearances. You will be tremendously blessed by her latest book, *God, Are you Listening? I Need Help!* I highly recommend it!

—Greg Roth, Pastor/Missionary
Yorktown, VA

This book is a powerful teaching on speaking the Word of God in faith as you pray! Pastor Jo Anne Ramsay responds to her listeners' email requests with teaching and personal prayer. She makes each person feel valued and welcomed as she answers your questions. I highly recommend this book to anyone wanting to learn how to pray with faith and power!

—Prophet Richard L. Spangler
Lion's Voice Ministries, Chesapeake, VA

Pastor Jo Ramsay is one of the most faithful and fervent prayer warriors that I know. She believes in God's Word and the power that comes from praying it. The personal testimonies and practical instruction in this book can be a guide to anyone desiring to improve their personal prayer life, or in need of a miracle for a situation that may seem impossible. If you read this book, you will be blessed mightily by it and will find the freedom and power you need.

—Dr. Tim Reaves, Lead Pastor
Pine Valley United Methodist Church, Wilmington, NC

God, Are You Listening?
I Need Help!

GOD, ARE YOU LISTENING?

I NEED HELP!

PASTOR JOANNE RAMSAY

Fruitbearer Publishing LLC
Georgetown, DE

Copyright © 2020 by JoAnne Ramsay. All rights reserved.
ISBN: 978-1-938796-62-3
Library of Congress Control Number: 2020902544
Cover Design: Candy Abbott (www.fruitbearer.com)
Published by Fruitbearer Publishing
P.O. Box 777
Georgetown, DE 19947
www.fruitbearer.com

Contents

Preface

It's possible that you picked up this book, or someone gave you a copy, yet you've never received Jesus as your Savior. He loves you! From the beginning, God's longing has been to have a family. We are not born again by natural birth. To be born again means to receive Jesus as your Savior from all sins you ever did, and to be born into God's family. Did you know that God loves you and He wants you to be His child, even now? "For God so loved the world that He gave His only begotten Son, that whoever believes in Him should not perish but have everlasting life" (John 3:16).

When you believe that Jesus is the Son of God and receive Jesus Christ as your Lord and Savior, you become a new person, a new being inside. Your body may look the same, but your spirit and soul inside of you will feel glorious!

Sin hurts, and our own sins can send us to hell, but God said that He is not willing that anyone should perish. When you accept Jesus as your Savior, you will begin living the life that Jesus died for you to live. You will live a life that is filled with His presence, and know that He will never leave you.

The Bible says that if you confess with your mouth that Jesus is Lord and you believe in your heart that God raised Him from the dead, you will be saved. "For with the heart one believes unto righteousness; and with the mouth confession is made unto salvation" (Romans 10:9, 10). "For whosoever shall call upon the name of the Lord shall be saved" (Romans 10:13 KJV).

Choosing Jesus as your Savior and being born again from above will be the most important decision you will ever make. If you are ready to receive Jesus as your Lord, please pray this prayer with me:

Father, I am sorry for my sins, every single thing I've done wrong. I believe Jesus died to forgive me, and I receive that forgiveness. Jesus, I make You my Lord. I believe that You are alive and that You now live in me. I am saved. I am forgiven. I thank You, Father, that I am now your child. In Jesus' name, Amen.

If you prayed that prayer and believe it in your heart, you are born again! You will look the same on the outside, but you are now a whole new person. Your spirit is now *alive* with the life of God and *ready* to enter heaven one day! You have been set free from the powers of darkness and delivered into the kingdom of God's dear Son, Jesus (see Colossians 1:13).

Email me at speakthewordministry@cox.net and I'll send you free audio messages to help you get started in your new life with God.

Introduction

Our enemy believes himself to be invincible. Yet when you and I discover the secrets of prayer and appropriate the powers of prayer, we will move against the enemies of God with an assurance and effectiveness we have never known. "Those who wait upon the Lord shall renew their strength; they shall mount up with wings like eagles, they shall run and not be weary, they shall walk and not faint" (Isaiah 40:31).

My point is this: Prayer has no equal and the power of prayer never changes. It stands when all other powers fail. There is no need to ever be afraid. God says He hears us always and He always answers. "Now this is the confidence that we have in Him, that if we ask anything according to His will, He hears us" (1 John 5:14).

God listens to you just as much as he listens to me—maybe more! As Christians, you and I are anointed by God to pray for anybody and lay hands on anybody to pray for them. Even so, I talk to many people in pain or financial hardship, who say they've been praying and praying, but not getting any answers. Why?

After talking to them, I realize they aren't getting answers because they are not praying in line with the Word of God. I pray for people over the phone and on email every week, and I'm seeing miracles happen all the time. If I return a call from a listener to my radio program and pray over them, or I reply to an email prayer request, I get results. Why? For one thing, before I respond to the request, I pray first and ask God how to pray so that I can speak or type an effective prayer.

Second, the Lord says in Hebrews to come to Him with boldness. A lot of times people pray and they're begging. You don't have to beg God. It's ours. It belongs to us. The Word of God says, "Let us therefore come *boldly* to the throne of grace, that we may obtain mercy and find grace to help in time of need" (Hebrews 4:16); "So we may *boldly* say: 'The Lord is my helper; I will not fear. What can man do to me?'" (Hebrews 13:6).

Third, I think there are so many people who need prayer but they don't read the Bible and don't know the Word. If it's in the Scriptures, it's a fact, a promise, and God will back up His Word.

Do you want your prayers answered? I believe you picked up this book because God led you to read it. He is about to bless your life and your prayers with His mighty power! Let me pray for you before you turn the page:

Father, I thank You for this wonderful person that You've sent to read these pages and be fed Your Word, Your testimonies, and Your thoughts on prayer. I ask You to open up their ears and to open the eyes of their heart to hear what You have to say, page by page, Lord. I pray that they will grasp only the words that You inspire. Father, I pray that when they consider Pastor Jo as the author that they will not see me but they will see You. Lord, I don't want to be seen. I want You to be seen. I want You to be felt. I know that Your presence is not about feelings—but it is so awesome to know that when we have Your presence, Lord, that we can feel it. So, Father God, in Jesus' name, I pray that the person reading this prayer will experience Your presence in a real and tangible way right now. It's Your presence, not mine, that we need. Father, I thank You for what You're about to do in my friend's life today. Thank You, Jesus. I praise You, Father! Hallelujah!

First Things First

But when you are praying, first forgive anyone you're holding a grudge against, so that your Father in heaven will forgive your sins, too.

Mark 11:25 NLT

Jesus said in the passage above that when we pray we are to *first* forgive any person who has hurt or offended us. If Jesus said to do something *first*, then we need to pay attention to it. Let's keep first things first!

I recently received an email from a mother that I will call Jen, who said,

Dear Pastor Jo,

Please pray for me. My daughter stopped talking to me . . .

Jen

I sent an email back to Jen and typed a prayer, asking God to restore her relationship with her daughter and to heal their hearts. Jen went on to explain the family circumstances that created hurt, confusion, and breakdown in her relationship with her daughter. I won't share the details, but we all know that relationships with people inside or outside our families can be difficult, and that sometimes it's not easy to forgive.

1

In fact, no one knows that better than our Lord Jesus. He hung there naked on the cross with people jeering at him and mocking Him. What did He say? He said, "Father, forgive them, for they don't know what they are doing" (Luke 23:34 NLT).

I encouraged Jen to forgive as Jesus forgave, and we agreed together for God to touch her daughter's heart with new love and forgiveness, and to restore their relationship. God answered our prayers! Hallelujah! Jen later wrote,

Dear Pastor Jo,

Praise report! My daughter reached out to me yesterday. The blindfolds came off and she said sorry and she loves me. I passed your website on to my daughter. What a blessing you are! Thank you for sharing with us how to pray and how to defeat the devil. God bless you and your family.

Jen

Do you see the forgiveness that was exchanged in this relationship? Jesus forgave each one of us our sins, so He requires that we forgive each other when we go to Him in prayer.

As a matter of fact, it is dangerous to your health if you do not forgive. It's especially damaging to your heart. Here are just a few of the dangers to your heart and circulation system that come from unforgiveness, resentment, and bitterness:

1. Hypertension
2. High blood pressure
3. Angina (chest pressure or pain)
4. Increased heart rate
5. Strokes (clogged blood vessels cause brain tissues to become oxygen-starved)

If you don't want to forgive for any other reason, forgive for your own health's sake. Your heart is only one of the systems in the body that is in danger.

Resentment, bitterness, lack of forgiveness, and self-hatred are just some of the toxic, negative thoughts and emotions that can trigger immune system disorders. Think about that. Jesus didn't mince words when He said, "But when you are praying, *first* forgive" (Mark 11:25).

Before we say a word to God in prayer, our hearts have to be right. If a hindrance or obstacle is delaying your prayer request, ask God if there is someone you need to forgive. If you are holding a grudge against someone, your prayer is going to hit the wall and get no further. So if we're holding a grudge against anyone, the Lord says, "Let it go." I know, sometimes it's not easy to forgive others, even those we love the most.

Let's look at this Scripture in the full context of what Jesus was teaching his disciples about prayer:

> Then Jesus said to the disciples, "Have faith in God. I tell you the truth, you can say to this mountain, 'May you be lifted up and thrown into the sea,' and it will happen. But you must really believe it will happen and have no doubt in your heart. I tell you, you can pray for anything, and if you believe that you've received it, it will be yours. But when you are praying, first forgive anyone you are holding a grudge against, so that your Father in heaven will forgive your sins, too. (Mark 11:22–25)

God is serious about this matter of forgiveness.

Perhaps you are familiar with the trials of Joseph in the book of Genesis. It says in Genesis 37 that right after Joseph had shared his dream with his brothers, they got angry with him and plotted to kill him. Once they caught him, instead of killing him right away, they stripped him of his clothing, took off his coat of many colors, and threw him into a pit.

But it gets worse! I read this Scripture several times because it's hard to believe your own family could be so mean. Genesis 37:25 says, "And they sat down to eat a meal."

Can you imagine that? They took their own brother, stripped him of all his clothing, tossed him into a pit—and then proceeded to sit down and eat lunch! That's cold. That's *bitter* cold. I can't imagine anyone being *that* cold and callous. We know, however, that instead of killing Joseph, they sold him to a group of Ishmaelites for twenty pieces of silver. Genesis 39:1 says that the Ishmaelites brought Joseph down to Egypt; Potiphar, an officer of Pharaoh, bought Joseph.

I love the next verse in this chapter! It says, "The LORD was with Joseph, so he succeeded in everything he did as he served in the home of his Egyptian master" (Genesis 39:2 NLT).

Can you imagine this? Here is a man stripped of his clothing and sold into slavery, yet God called him successful and prosperous. Think about that! I want you to get another picture in your mind now: Potiphar stood there, arrayed like Solomon in all his glory, in fine gold and linen, while Joseph stood there naked. And God called *Joseph* blessed, not Potiphar. God didn't see Potiphar as prosperous. It gives you different perspective as to what is successful and what's not. There's more. It says in 39:3, "And his master saw that the LORD was with him and the LORD made all he did to prosper in his hand." Potiphar trusted Joseph.

But Potiphar's wife was another matter. Potiphar's wife tried to get Joseph to have sex with her. Joseph refused. Joseph did the right thing, but Potiphar's wife lied about him and convinced her husband to throw Joseph into prison. Sometimes you get in trouble for doing what is right. Hang on, child of God! The Lord has a plan for your deliverance out of trouble and into Kingdom promotion! But first, like Joseph, you will need to learn forgiveness. Let's see what Joseph's prison life looked like:

Then Joseph's master took him and put him into the prison, a place where the king's prisoners were confined. And he was

there in the prison. But the LORD was with Joseph and showed him mercy, and He gave him favor in the sight of the keeper of the prison. And the keeper of the prison committed to Joseph's hand all the prisoners who were in the prison; whatever they did there, it was his doing. The keeper of the prison did not look into anything that was under Joseph's authority, because the LORD was with him; and whatever he did, the LORD made it prosper. (Genesis 39:20–24)

We see that in Potiphar's house, Joseph succeeded in all he did. While in prison, the Lord was with him and made all that Joseph did to prosper. Prosperity and success is wonderful, but Joseph was a slave in one place and a prisoner in the other! I don't know about you, but I would have a hard time forgiving people by this time.

You can read for yourself in Genesis 40 how two prisoners had dreams and Joseph interpreted the dreams, with God's help. When the interpretation to the dreams came to be true, Joseph asked the one prisoner, the king's cupbearer, to remember him before Pharaoh. Joseph wanted to get out of prison! "Pharaoh's chief cup-bearer, however, forgot all about Joseph, never giving him another thought" (Genesis 40:23 NLT).

Joseph had a dream from God as a boy. In Joseph's dream, God showed him that one day many people, including his family members, would bow to him like a king. But in order for Joseph to lay hold of the promise of God, he had to first forgive all the people who hurt him. Think about that. Look what Joseph went through!

1. His family betrayed him and sold him into slavery.
2. His employer's wife lied to her husband and said Joseph tried to force her to have sex.
3. His employer, Potiphar, believed his wife's lie, and had Joseph thrown into prison.
4. Joseph correctly interpreted two dreams in prison but was forgotten.

GOD, ARE YOU LISTENING?

How could Joseph forgive so many people? Would he ever get to the promise of God? Well, I'll get back to Joseph in a minute. First, let's think about you and me.

God tells us in Proverbs 18:21 that the power of life lies in our tongue. I'm sure Joseph could have used his tongue to give a good tongue-lashing to all the people who had hurt him. Joseph could have been bitter, but he chose to keep his mouth shut. Sometimes that is hard because your flesh is just itching, really itching hard to say something! It's not always easy to keep a zipper on it, but you have to do it.

The day finally came when Joseph's true feelings came to the forefront. After correctly interpreting the Pharaoh's dream, Joseph was made second-in-command in all of Egypt. One day his brothers came to Egypt to buy food during the terrible famine. Joseph recognized his brothers, but his brothers didn't recognize him. Joseph was dressed in royal Egyptian clothing and sat on a throne, second only to Pharoah!

Do you think that Joseph forgot that his brothers stripped him of his clothes and threw him into a pit? Do you think Joseph had any feelings for them at all? Let's read from Scripture about the day when Joseph revealed himself to his brothers:

Joseph could stand it no longer. There were many people in the room, and he said to his attendants, "Out, all of you!" So he was alone with his brothers when he told them who he was. Then *he broke down and wept. He wept so loudly the Egyptians could hear him*, and word of it quickly carried to Pharaoh's palace.

"I am Joseph!" he said to his brothers. "Is my father still alive?" But his brothers were speechless! They were stunned to realize that Joseph was standing there in front of them. "Please, come closer," he said to them. So they came closer. And he said again, "I am Joseph, your brother, whom you sold into slavery in Egypt. *But don't be upset, and don't be angry with yourselves for selling me to this place. It was God who sent me here ahead of you to preserve your lives.* This famine that has ravaged the land for two years will last five more years, and there will be neither plowing nor harvesting. God has sent me ahead of you to keep you and your families alive and to preserve many survivors. So it was God who sent me here, not you! And he is the one who made me an adviser to Pharaoh—the manager of his entire palace and the governor of all Egypt." (Genesis 45:1–8 NLT)

You know, this could have been Joseph's moment to tell his brothers off. Was he emotional? You bet he was emotional! Joseph had been extremely hurt. Imagine lying naked in a pit right next to your brothers as they sat down to eat their lunch. Imagine being sold off to total strangers as your brothers walked away. Imagine never seeing your father, the one person you were closest to in all the world, for years and years. Joseph had reason to be bitter, but instead he chose to see God's hand in all of it. In fact, he told his brothers, "Don't be upset, and don't be angry with yourselves for selling me." Now, that's complete forgiveness!

Joseph showed more concern, love, and compassion for his brothers than his brothers ever showed to him. Isn't that what love is all about? Joseph showed us what true forgiveness looks like.

Remember, Jesus said when we pray we are to *first* forgive any person that has hurt us or offended us. Let's take time right now to forgive people that have hurt us. Pray this prayer out loud with me now:

Father, I thank You that when I became a child of Your kingdom You forgave me of all my sins—past, present and future—and that You no longer hold any of them against me. You said You have placed them as far as the east is from the west, to remember them no more. You said, Lord, that blessed is the man whose sin the Lord will NEVER count against him. Lord, I pray for the grace to forgive those who have sinned against me. Those who have offended me and caused me pain, I ask You to reaffirm Your love for them. And anyone whom You forgive, I also will forgive. I forgive those who have hurt me because I am strong enough to accept the fact that people make mistakes. By faith I forgive them, and by faith I believe that my feelings will catch up with my forgiveness. It's in YOUR hands, God. I pray that You would bless them. Amen.

—⟋⟍—

Chapter 2

Pray Where the Power Comes Out

Then they cried out to the Lord in their trouble, and He saved them out of their distresses. He sent His word and healed them, and delivered them from their destructions.

Psalm 107:19, 20

Did you ever see one of those commercials in which a person opens a book to read and a bright light floods their face, while the book seems to come alive? We need to picture the power of God coming into our countenance like that every time we open the Word of God. There is no book in the whole world that contains more power than the Bible. When you see a promise in the Word of God, pray it out! When God highlights a passage of Scripture to you, declare that promise over your situation. The Word of God is powerful!

Being a Christian does not mean that we'll never go through trials. Joseph's life shows us that even the most righteous person may endure hardship, but as God's child we are guaranteed that He will be with us and get us through our trouble. God is able to do anything, and He will bring us out.

GOD, ARE YOU LISTENING?

Perhaps you are in a trial right now as you are reading this book. It could be trouble in a job, it could in your health, it could be in your finances, or maybe something in your marriage or with your children. It's possible that in the natural, things aren't looking very good.

Remember this: Your battle is always a spiritual battle. It's never in the natural. And you cannot fight a spiritual battle any other way except with the Word of God. There is just no other way.

If the storm hits and you are in the right place, feeding on God's Word, then when it's all over you will not only survive like Joseph did, but you will thrive and be positioned in an even higher place. If you have God's Word in your heart, you're going to end up on top. It may not always look like it at first in the natural, but you're going to end up in a higher place.

When God spoke, as written in Genesis 1, whatever he called forth came forth. Hebrews 11:3 says that the world was framed by the Word of God. God's words carry power and our words carry power, too. "If anyone speaks, let him speak as the oracles of God. If anyone ministers, let him do it as with the ability which God supplies, that in all things God may be glorified through Jesus Christ, to whom belong the glory and the dominion forever and ever. Amen" (1 Peter 4:11).

Hallelujah! God created us in His image and after His likeness. Our spoken words are powerful! When our prayers are released through declarations of praise, in faith, and with authority, it sends shock waves through the spirit realm. Do you understand that? When we speak God's Word in prayer, in song, in declaration, in conversation, those words send shock waves through the spirit realm and things are going to *move*! Instead of things moving you, God's Word coming out of your mouth is going to move those things. Glory to God!

God tells us in Isaiah 43:26 to put Him in remembrance of His Word that He may plead your case. God knows what He said in His Word, of course. He didn't forget what He said. God wants us to remember and believe what His Word says because His Word brings life to us when it's alive in our hearts. This is why He tells us to remind Him, put Him in remembrance of what He said, "Put Me in remembrance; / Let us contend together; / State your case, that you may be acquitted" (Isaiah 43:26).

Unless you are familiar with my teaching through YouTube or my conferences, then what I'm going to say next may shock you. But listen to this because it's in the Word of God. Your words will control your life and determine your future. Look what God said in Job 15:6 in *The New Living Translation* (NLT): "Your own mouth condemns you, not I. / Your own lips testify against you."

God says that the words that are coming out of our mouths are hurting us. He says, "You are snared by the words of your mouth" (Proverbs 6:2).

We can be snared by our own words. We may pray a wonderful, powerful prayer, but if we grumble and complain, we set a snare for our feet. Don't give the devil a foothold in your circumstances. If you let him, he will defeat you with your own words. Use your mouth for what it was created to do—praise God! Your mouth was created to declare and decree what God says about you in His Word. Remember this: It is only what you say about you that will ever defeat you. It is only what I say about me that will ever defeat me.

You need to separate yourself from your thoughts and your feelings and say God's Word out loud. When you pray, don't whine or fuss at God and tell him how bad it is. What you think and what you feel does not change anything—not one iota.

God loves us and comforts us, but He does not take action based on our human thoughts or emotions. God is moved by His Word. Let me say that again because this is so important. God is moved by His Word. So if we want to pray effectively, we need to pray His Word. We cannot expect to receive a healing, a car, a house, a child, or a spouse from God if we don't feed on the Word. It's as simple as that. If we want to pray effectively, then we need to feed on the Word of God. We will be defeated by what comes out of our mouths or be blessed by what comes out of our mouths.

GOD, ARE YOU LISTENING?

I can promise you that if you will begin to monitor the words coming out of your mouth that the mountains that you are facing right now will come down. Decree this with me:

I decree and declare that God is moved by His Word. Beginning right now my mouth is a weapon that speaks the uncompromising, unstoppable Word of the Living God!

Child of God, you will never be defeated by what someone else says about you. You are only going to be defeated by what you say about yourself. When you write down a prayer or speak a prayer, you always want to back it up with God's Word because God's Word is where the power comes out.

"As for Me," says the Lord, "this is My covenant with them: My Spirit who is upon you, and my Word which I have put in your mouth, shall not depart from your mouth, nor from the mouth of your descendants, nor from the mouth of your descendants' descendants," says the Lord, "from this time and forevermore." (Isaiah 59:21)

The Lord wants you to experience more freedom in your life and also give you a better understanding of His Word. God has anointed you to take His Word and speak it over your situations—over your health, your finances, your relationships, your promotion at work, or whatever is going on in your life right now. Take the Word of God, which is called the Sword of the Spirit, and wield that sword by speaking the Word of God in prayer, praise, declaration, and even in your mind and thoughts.

I want to be honest with you here: I am not a praying superstar! Sometimes I pray and my prayers seem cold. You probably know what I'm talking about. But it doesn't matter, because you don't base your prayers, your praise, or your faith on your feelings. Don't ever base your

faith on your feelings. Faith must be based on the Word of God. God says that He is with you always; that He will never leave you. Now either He is or He isn't! But He is. If He says He is, He is.

If you've been born again and received Christ as your Savior, you know that he cleans your heart and saves you. It can feel wonderful. Five years down the road you may not feel so wonderful. Just the other day I was taking communion and I prayed, *God, I just thank You that my salvation is not based on my feelings. I thank You, Lord, that my strength is not based on my feelings. I just thank You that none of it is based on my feelings. I know that You are here, whether I feel like You are here or not.*

This is what we have to do. Truthfully, if we could just get our feelings out of the way, we could get a whole lot further down the road. You know, the devil is the one that does that to us. He gets us thinking about how we feel. He even suggests to us that we should feel worse than we did a minute ago! Don't listen to him. Cast down those suggestions that come to your mind and speak the Word of God instead!

Not everything that is bad for us comes from the devil. The Bible tells us that our own heart is a most deceitful thing, and sometimes it will lie to us. We can't trust it. We can't trust our feelings as being the truth. Our feelings are going to lie to us, but God's Word will never lie. When we pray, we need to speak God's Word over our situation and God will act! God always acts upon His Word when it is spoken with faith from our mouths.

You and I get a lot of opportunities every day to declare God's Word over our circumstances. Depending on whether we choose to say what God's Word has to say over our circumstances, or what Satan is telling us to think and say, is really going to determine the outcome. It's our choice. It is whatever we choose. The Lord puts it this way: "Today I have given you the choice between life and death, between blessings and curses. Now I call on heaven and earth to witness the choice that you make. Oh, that you would choose life, so that you and your descendants might live" (Deuteronomy 30:29 NLT).

GOD, ARE YOU LISTENING?

If we go to God in prayer and just talk about how we feel, we will get nowhere. Now there is a place to tell God how we feel and speak to Him as our Father and our best friend. But telling God that something or someone hurt us is a lot different than whining and fussing. God has no interest in participating in a pity party or temper tantrum! Remember, negative words will bring curses and they always equal death. However, Jesus tells us that His words are spirit and life: "It is the Spirit who gives life; the flesh profits nothing. The words that I speak to you are spirit, and they are life" (John 6:63).

Prayer is speaking life! I know that it might sound just a little crazy to you at first when you look at lifeless things or things you can't see in the natural and start calling them alive and active, but that's what God's Word says: "God, who gives life to the dead and calls those things which do not exist as though they did" (Romans 4:17b).

When you speak life in your prayer, people may think that you are radical! They may think you are crazy. Let me give you a personal example. I had a palm tree that was dying and I laid hands on it. It's a living thing and I spoke life over that tree.

The man who takes care of our yard said, "Well, Mrs. Ramsay, I think we are going to have to take that one out."

"I don't think so," I answered.

He said, "Well, we will give it a few weeks."

I agreed to that and then a little bit later I noticed another one of my trees by my driveway, and that tree looked really sad. We thought maybe it was thirsty. I told my husband and he started dumping buckets of water on it. I went out there one morning and it had dead leaves, so I took the clippers and I cut all the dead leaves off.

I laid my hands on that plant and I said, "Plant, I am speaking to you in the name of Jesus! I declare that you shall live and not die. I declare you shall bear much good fruit."

God spoke to everything and you and I are created in his image and his likeness, so He has given us His ability to speak. Let them think you are radical!

A couple weeks later, the man who tends our yard came back. I said, "You know that bush over there that you said was dead? It ain't dead." (I know that's poor English, but that's what I said.)

The man agreed. "It's living," he said.

I like to declare life over the plants and trees in my yard! For example, about two years ago we lost about four palm trees because the weather was so cold. It saddened me to look out my bathroom window and see nothing but four brown stubs in the ground. So I walked across my yard and I said, "Everything that grows here is going to live. You are growing on anointed ground!"

Now, God is my witness. When I looked out my window one morning soon afterward, those palm trees had leaves on them! The Lord says you can speak to anything. I speak to anything. I speak to my body. I speak to plants. I speak to my vehicle when it won't go.

My dishwasher wasn't working. My husband called the handyman, and I said, "You don't need the handyman." I said, "Dishwasher, I speak to you in the name of Jesus, and I command you to function as you were designed and created to function—now, in the name of Jesus. Father, I just thank you for the ability that you have given me to speak."

I turned it on and it ran. Whoo hoo!

My point is that we can pray about anything and everything. Perhaps your concern today isn't a large problem in your finances or your health. Maybe it's something as simple as a car that won't start. Speak to it. You have been given authority and power.

Jesus never prayed the problem; he always prayed the solution. God created with His Word, and you can create with your words, too. As a matter of fact, you have already been confessing things with your mouth. You've already been creating with your mouth.

We can create things that we don't want with our mouth. There is power in the spoken Word of God and there is power in the human tongue, too. "Death and life are in the power of the tongue, / And those who love it will eat its fruit" (Proverbs 18:21).

We should speak the things we love and want in our lives. Instead, sometimes we speak the things that we don't want. We can repeat a fear expressed by someone else and just like that, we speak poverty over our lives. Or we can speak sickness over our body. Remember, Jesus taught us that our words are like seeds. What you plant will come up! Jesus puts it this way. He said that the kingdom of God works like a seed. A seed always produces after its kind according to Genesis 1:11. And according to Luke 8:11 the seed is the Word of God. And just like the seed does nothing until it is planted, so God's Word is activated by you giving voice to it.

Let's look at what Jesus said about the seeds that are planted: "The Kingdom of God is like a farmer who scatters seed on the ground. Night and day, while he's asleep or awake, the seed sprouts and grows, but he does not understand how it happens" (Mark 4:26, 27 nlt).

The seed works day and night so, whether you are asleep or awake, Jesus says the seed sprouts and grows, but you know not how. In other words, if you have been praying God's Word into your loved ones' lives, your job, your home, and your ministry, but you still don't see the harvest coming up—*wait!*

Please don't give up, child of God. That seed is working. Some seed just takes a little bit longer to grow. I've seen people plant winter ryegrass along the beach in Virginia and only five days later it was very tall! But not everything happens that way. Some seeds take a little longer to come up.

The seeds I plant with my words in prayer and declaration sprout up at different times. Some take days, some months, and some even years, but they will come up. My friend, let's plant some seeds together right now! Pray this prayer out loud with me:

Father, I come to You in the name of Jesus, and I pray a special blessing over my family, my finances, my health, and my ministry. I ask that, just as You were with Joseph, You will be with me. I thank You, Lord, that my strength is not based on my feelings. I know that You are here, whether I feel like You are here or not. I know that You are fully aware of all the things that concern me, for You said all the things that concern me concern You. You care about me. Thank You for loving me.

Father God, I put You in remembrance of Your Word and state my case. I choose life and blessings over each situation that I am facing right now. I determine in my heart to speak Your Word. Lord, You are the one who gives life to the dead, and You tell me to do the same. I speak life to the dead and dark places around me and I call into existence the life of God. The good seeds I have planted will come up! I will have a harvest of life according to the Word of God. I set my hope, my faith, and my love upon You, Lord. You move when Your Word is spoken so I ask that, beginning right now, my mouth will be a weapon that speaks the uncompromising, unstoppable Word of the Living God!

Holy Spirit, I call on You to help me pray effectively, to lead me, and to teach me. I thank You that according to Your Word You are my Teacher and my Helper. I ask this in the name of Jesus, who gives life to the dead and calls those things which do not exist as though they did. Hallelujah! Amen.

—⟶⟵—

Chapter 3

Help! I Need Money

And my God shall supply all your need according to His riches in glory by Christ Jesus.

Philippians 4:19

Remember the Lord your God. He is the one who gives you the power to be successful, in order to fulfill the covenant he confirmed to your ancestors with an oath.

Deuteronomy 8:18 NLT

D id you know that 75% of the emails and phone calls I get every day are prayer requests for financial difficulties? Some people can't pay their rent. Recently, I received an email from a lady who needed money to pay her light bill, her car payment, her insurance, and toiletries—I mean, she needed it all.

When your finances are in disarray, it can be overwhelming. And sometimes debt can accumulate through no fault of our own. One debt I had for over $35,000 was my own doing, because I didn't use wisdom. But God still helped me, and he will help you, too! We don't always use wisdom. None of us have it down perfectly.

GOD, ARE YOU LISTENING?

I remember a time shortly after the Lord paid off one debt for me, that I received another bill for almost $100,000. It was from the hospital my husband was in before he passed away. Of course, that bill was not my doing, but nevertheless I still had to pay it. Whether it is your doing or not, we still have to pay the bill, don't we? I want to tell you that just like God promised in His Word, He did rescue me in both of those situations. He rescued me when it was the result of my lack of wisdom, and he rescued me when it wasn't my fault.

If you are in trouble due to poor judgment on your part, God will still help you. If it wasn't your fault, He will still help you. A lot of people think God is angry with them and won't answer their prayers for help. If you ever think that way, you need to write this Scripture down somewhere, read it, and re-read it every now and then: "Just as I swore in the time of Noah / that I would never again let a flood cover the earth, / so now I swear / that I will never again be angry and punish you" (Isaiah 54:9 NLT).

Hallelujah! God is not up there judging you, whether it was your fault or not. The only thing He wants you to do is ask Him, and then trust that He will help you. The only thing that ties God's hands is us putting limitations on Him. Don't limit God! Don't let yourself carry guilt over a poor decision you made in the past. God forgives; God restores. Take that decision to the cross and leave it there. Trust God to turn your situation around from this day forward.

Aren't you glad that God forgives? Aren't you blessed because He tenderly loves you? There's not one of us on this planet who gets it right every time. We all need God.

Jesus described Himself as the Good Shepherd in John, chapter 10: "I am the good shepherd; I know my own sheep, and they know me, just as my Father knows me and I know the Father. So I sacrifice my life for the sheep" (John 10:14, 15 NLT).

That old devil is just the opposite. Satan steals, kills, and destroys. Let's look at what Jesus had to say about our enemy, the devil: "The thief's purpose is to steal and kill and destroy. My purpose is to give them a rich and satisfying life" (John 10:10 NLT).

I recall one prayer request from a woman named Cindy, whose daughter needed a financial breakthrough, when it seemed the devil did all he could to rob from an entire company!

Hi Pastor Jo,

I would appreciate it if you would pray with me for my oldest daughter, Bella. Everything in her life for some time now has been going wrong. She just informed me that she and sixty other employees lost their jobs yesterday. She's a single mother trying to provide for her son and herself. She needs a new job, a good job making the amount she was making or more. I pray that she would see God's goodness and His love for her.

Thank you so much for all you do.

Sincerely,

Cindy

I prayed with Cindy, using a prayer much like the one you will read at the end of this chapter. I heard back from her weeks later. Her daughter got a new job that was a great blessing to her!

God didn't come into Cindy's daughter's life to steal her job and the jobs of sixty other employees. The devil is the one who steals. I like to think of it this way: Satan is the giant termite. Use the exterminator!

Brother Lester Sumrall used to say that the termites in the Philippines could eat through a wall until there was nothing left except a thin veneer, as thin as a man's shirt. The termites ate the rest of it up. I got a close-up picture of the damage that can be done by termites when I put my home in North Carolina on the market.

When the home was inspected, they found a lot of termite damage. I had to have someone come in, tear out practically half my living room floor, and replace it with all new wood because of the damage that the termites had done. Not only that, but I had to pay somebody to come in and treat what the termites had done. It got to be kind of expensive.

I'm not talking necessarily about the termites and the damage in my home. My point is that Satan is much like a termite. He likes to slowly eat away at our lives. Every day he is just slowly eating away. He will slowly steal from you and rob you blind. Sadly, some people aren't even aware that the devil and his demons are the thieves. They don't even realize that the devil and his demons are the ones responsible for all their losses.

As long as there are termites in your house, you have to work to exterminate them. In the same way, as long as we are on this earth, we have to fight the devil. Satan is a cultural termite—wouldn't you agree? He is slowly eating away at our very civilization, and you and I are the only exterminators that God has. We must begin to exercise our God-given authority and become fighters and destroyers of Satan's evil works.

Jesus says in John 3:8 that he came to destroy the works of the devil. As children of God you and I have been anointed to help destroy the works of the devil, too. When you accept Jesus as your Lord and Savior, you become anointed to help Him destroy the works of robbing and stealing from God's children.

Think about this: You never see termites on the surface because their business is underneath. Isn't that just like the devil? Sometimes you don't see him coming until he has already done the damage.

In the natural, termites do not look like they could possibly be that destructive or do so much damage. Their bodies may be soft and delicate, but they are strong enough to eat a house. I can witness to that. If you had seen pictures of my house with half my floor torn out, you would know that they could do some damage. Left alone, they could have destroyed the whole house. We had to replace two walls in our guest house because termites had come in and we didn't know they were there. We discovered the termites by accident while trying to hang a picture. If it had gone unnoticed the whole thing would have fallen down.

That's the way Satan is. If he goes unnoticed, he will wipe out your whole life and you won't even know what happened until it is gone.

I'm sure you didn't know you were going to get an education on termites when reading a chapter on finances! But please allow me to take this one step further. Did you know that adult termites develop wings so that they can leave the colony and find a new home? They destroy and then help the termite populations grow. Isn't that what Satan does too? Look at this Scripture with me:

> When an evil spirit leaves a person, it goes into the desert, searching for rest. But when it finds none, it says, "I will return to the person I came from." So it returns and finds that its former home is all swept and in order. Then the spirit finds seven other spirits more evil than itself, and they all enter the person and live there. And so that person is worse off than before. (Luke 11:24–26 NLT)

Jesus said that a person can get set free and, if that person is not careful, Satan will bring back seven more evil spirits that are even worse than the one that the person got set free from!

We need to understand how this termite, the devil, operates: "Even Satan disguises himself as an angel of light. So it is no wonder that his servants also disguise themselves as servants of righteousness. In the end they will get the punishment their wicked deeds deserve" (2 Corinthians 11:14, 15 NLT).

Satan disguises himself as an angel of light and all his little demons work for him. What does that mean to you and me? That means that Satan will always present sin to you as something pleasing and beautiful. He tempts us to sin, yet makes that sin look like something to be desired and to be looked upon. He comes as an angel of light. He will never come up to you with something you will recognize as a termite, eating away the walls of your home! He comes in a form that you won't recognize because he is very subtle. He presents false teachings as enlightening and life-changing. He is very deceptive. The only way that he can conquer you is by deceiving you, so he always comes to you in a way that is deceitful.

We need to start acting like heirs of the kingdom of heaven. In heaven there is no lack. We need to serve notice on the devil and let him know that he no longer has any claim on us, that he is a defeated foe. I believe it is safe to say that there is no one alive that can honestly say that he has not stolen something from them, including myself. Maybe you've had your finances stolen. If he can get away with it, Satan will wipe out all you own. But I'm here to say that it's time to get it back!

I say you can get back what was stolen if you can identify the thief. I just showed you that John 10:10 says that the thief comes to steal, kill, and destroy, but Jesus came to give us a rich and satisfying life. Look at this Scripture:

> Excuses might be found for a thief
> who steals because he is starving.
> But if he is caught, he must pay back seven times what he stole,
> even if he has to sell everything in his house.
>
> (Proverbs 6:30, 31 NLT)

That is the Word. It is written that if you can identify the thief, he has to give it back to you seven times over. I got a hold of this verse as a promise from God in my own personal life. Back in 2008, the Lord brought this verse to my remembrance one day. I used to have a place on the water, but the devil stole it from me right after my husband passed away. That beach house used to be where I spent my time with the Lord, worshipping the Lord, meditating on the Word, and doing my work. I'd go there to prepare for what the Lord called me to do, but the enemy stole it away from me.

So I had this conversation with God. He brought this verse back to my remembrance—Proverbs 6:31. I wrote down the Scripture and I said, "Lord, you said that if a person could identify the thief, that he will have to repay me seven times. Lord, the devil stole from me and Jim (my deceased husband). He stole our beach home. So I command you, Satan, to return to me seven times what you stole from me, in Jesus' name. I mean, I want a place with lots of rooms for my children and a nice yard for my flowers. Lord, based on your Holy Word, I fully expect to have returned to me a beachfront property seven times bigger and better than the one he stole." That's what I wrote.

I can tell you that God has given me a beautiful place on the water with rooms that I asked for. I have a beautiful yard with lots of flowers, and a place on the water where you can fish off my deck. My office overlooks the water and all the boats as they go by. Hallelujah! That was so much better than the mobile home on the beach. And look at the ministry he has blessed me with! I already had a ministry and he has quadrupled it.

God is good, and I can't praise him enough.

The devil wants to strip you of your identity. He wants to strip you of everything—but he can't do it. He tries, though, and he will if you let him, but only if you let him. The Word says in Romans 2:11 that God does not show favoritism. No one of us is different than another. God's desire is that you prosper and lack nothing. In order for God to help you with your finances, you need to start agreeing with him and trusting in his name. Exercise your power and your authority. There is no other way.

You are going to have to start fasting from those thoughts of doubt and from those negative words that you've been speaking and from those thoughts of failure and defeat. You can't be thinking thoughts of failure and defeat and get ahead. It just doesn't work that way. Job 6:24 says, "Teach me and I will hold my tongue; / Cause me to understand wherein I have erred." David said in Psalms 39:1, "I will guard my ways / lest I sin with my tongue; / I will restrain my mouth with a muzzle, / while the wicked are before me."

GOD, ARE YOU LISTENING?

Your voice gives life to the Word. The Word of God is active and sharper than any two-edged sword. He says it will cut through bone and marrow, even to the dividing of spirit and soul.

If you need finances right now, say this with me: "The Lord supplies all my needs according to his riches in glory by Christ Jesus. He is my Provider."

We have to stop poor-mouthing. In the south, that means that we need to stop whining and complaining about our lack. Don't blame some circumstance or some person for your problems, either.

I recently received an email from a gentleman that said, "Sister, I am so broke that I just sleep all day long. I just lay around all day long, worrying and fretting." That person is not going to get anything. I send people verses, CDs, and prayers. Sometimes I have other little books that I buy to send people. I do what I can, and I pray for them, but they have to do something. They have to take authority. It doesn't matter who or what you used to be before you were born again because now you are a new creature in Christ Jesus according to 2 Corinthians 5:17. If any man be in Christ, he is a new creature altogether. Old things have passed away and all things have become new. It really doesn't matter who or what you used to be.

First John 3:8 says that Jesus came to destroy the works of the devil and this spirit of poverty is the work of the devil.

I know one person who needed a job and an apartment. Somehow, their application for the apartment got thrown into the trash can! That person kept believing for the apartment anyway and just kept glorifying God, kept thanking the Lord. Somehow or other, that application miraculously got moved out of that trash can and about a week later, they got the apartment! In fact, they told me that the apartment was the best one available. You just cannot imagine what God wants to do for us, but we first have to honor Him and praise Him for what He has already done—not wait until such-and-such happens, but just praise Him now.

PASTOR JOANNE RAMSAY

I want to give you some Scriptures you can meditate on. It's important that you always agree with the Lord and not the devil, no matter what it looks like. Even if things get worse for awhile—and sometimes it will—*don't stop saying what the Word says.* Know that God is working, whether You see Him or not.

> The blessing of the LORD makes a person rich,
>   and he adds no sorrow with it.
>
> (Proverbs 10:22 NLT)

> Excuses might be found for a thief
>   who steals because he is starving.
> But if he is caught, he must pay back seven times what he stole,
>   even if he has to sell everything in his house.
>
> (Proverbs 6:30, 31 NLT)

> Submit to God, and you will have peace;
>   then things will go well for you.
> Listen to his instructions,
>   and store them in your heart.
>
> (Job 22:21–22 NLT)

> Those who control their tongue will have a long life;
>   opening your mouth can ruin everything.
>
> (Proverbs 13:3 NLT)

> You will succeed in whatever you choose to do,
>   and light will shine on the road ahead of you.
>
> (Job 22:28 NLT)

GOD, ARE YOU LISTENING?

If you openly declare that Jesus is Lord and believe in your heart that God raised him from the dead, you will be saved. (Romans 10:9 NLT)

> But in that coming day
> no weapon turned against you will succeed.
> You will silence every voice
> raised up to accuse you.
> These benefits are enjoyed by the servants of the LORD;
> their vindication will come from me.
> I, the LORD, have spoken!
>
> (Isaiah 54:17 NLT)

Wealth and honor come from you alone, for you rule over everything. Power and might are in your hand, and at your discretion people are made great and given strength. (1 Chronicles 29:12 NLT)

And my God shall supply all your need according to His riches in glory by Christ Jesus. (Philippians 4:19)

If you listen to these commands of the Lord your God that I have given you today, and if you carefully obey them, the Lord will make you the head and not the tail, and you will always be on top and never on the bottom. (Deuteronomy 28:13 NLT)

Do you want to experience power coming out of your voice? Read those Scriptures above. Read them out loud! You can also remind the Lord that you pay your tithes. Remind Him that He promised to open the windows of heaven and pour out a blessing on you that you would not have room to contain it all. See what God promises to those who give

Him the first ten percent of their income: "'Bring all the tithes into the storehouse so there will be enough food in my Temple. If you do,' says the Lord of Heaven's Armies, 'I will open the windows of heaven for you. I will pour out a blessing so great you won't have enough room to take it in! Try it! Put me to the test!'" (Malachi 3:10 NLT).

Do you remember when Jesus healed the lepers? (See Luke 17:11–19) All that leprosy left their bodies. Picture that. Now you can pray:

Father, I thank You that just as the leprosy got up and left the lepers of old, so has all my debt got up and left me, in the name of Jesus.

You can get up in the morning and say, "Glory to God! My debt got up and left me, in Jesus' name!"

Wait! We're not finished yet! I want to help you pray right now and get a breakthrough in your finances.

God, Your Word says that whatever I bind on earth is bound in heaven and whatever I loose on earth is loosed in heaven. Therefore, on the authority of Your Word, I now bind every force that has set itself against my financial prosperity!

Based on Your Word, I have authority here on this earth and, according to Mark 11:23, I can speak to the mountain and it will have to obey me. You said that if I had faith (Luke 17:5–6) I would speak.

So therefore, devil, I speak to you and command you to take your hands off my finances right now in the name of Jesus. I speak to the mountain of lack and want and I command you to be removed and cast into the sea in the Name of Jesus.

I HEREBY DECLARE ALL CURSES AGAINST ME NULL, VOID, AND HARMLESS! I am redeemed from the curse of poverty! I am free from oppression! I now loose the abundance of God, and all that rightfully belongs to me now comes to me under grace in a perfect way.

I thank You Lord that You have a plan for me to overcome this financial adversity—this was no surprise to You. I cast all the problems of this situation over on You, Lord. I WILL NOT WORRY, and neither will I FRET.

Author's note: List the things where you need a financial miracle, such as mortgage, credit card, bills, etc. Put your bills in a stack. Lay your hands upon them, and declare out loud:

God supplies all my need according to His riches in glory by Christ Jesus. God is the source of my supply, and I have more than enough to pay my bills on time and more than enough left over to be a blessing to others.

No matter how big the mountain of debt is, it's not bigger than my God. I SPEAK to all my debt and I command it to be paid. Debt, I am speaking to you and telling you to be paid in full in the name of Jesus. Debts, be reduced and be eliminated. I call each one of my bills to be paid on time, paid in full, in the name of Jesus.

I thank You, Lord, that I don't have to figure out where the money is coming from, because that's Your concern. I have released my faith, now I shall receive my provision. I thank You, Lord, that if my income is not enough to cover all my expenses, then You will make up the difference.

God, I thank You that You are my provider, my deliverer, and my strong tower. Thank You, Lord, that the Holy Spirit gives me insight, wisdom, and favor to navigate my way through this adversity. Jesus will never leave me or abandon me. I will trust in the Lord and boast in His Word. I will patiently wait and see the salvation of the Lord. Amen.

Father, I thank You that as I give voice to Your Word, You are active and alert to perform it (Jeremiah 1:12). I declare that this is my time for increase, more and more.

I declare:

1. *My greatest barriers will come crashing down and a flood of God's presence will be all around.*

3. *God's goodness is outpoured, and every door that's been shut will be shut no more. Praise the Lord (Isaiah 22:22).*

4. *God's highest and greatest blessings for my family and me.*

5. *I will experience widespread increase in every area of my life.*

6. *My latter years are going to be much greater and more rewarding than my former years. Thank You, Lord, that You have saved the best for last.*

Praise Your Holy name, Lord. Amen and Amen.

CHAPTER 4

Faith for Healing

[Jesus] who Himself bore our sins in His own body on the tree . . . by whose stripes you were healed.

First Peter 2:24

I don't perform miracles, but God performs miracles. God performs miracles through our faith in His Word. When we truly hear the Word of God, the Lord can bring our faith level up high enough so that we can receive our healing. Now you and I both know that God has the power to heal every one of us! I want to take this chapter to build your faith so you can pray and receive your healing from the Lord.

But before I go any further on this topic, let me clarify this. There is absolutely nothing wrong with going to the doctor. I have a great respect for the medical profession. I have been to a doctor and if I need to go again, I will go. One good thing about going to doctors is that they can diagnose your sickness. Then you will know for sure what to pray about. When I'm praying over something, I like to be specific about what I'm praying for, whether it's a headache or toothache or a backache or whatever.

Going to the doctor doesn't mean that you have less faith. You can take that medication and mix it with your faith. You can say, "Lord, I know that I'm healed." Maybe you are still experiencing some symptoms, but you know that you are healed. I'm not advocating at all that you give up medicine or that you don't go to the doctor. I'm just saying there is a better way!

In fact, I want to share the testimony of a five-year-old girl who heard me teach on healing. I asked Kristina to share her testimony at a meeting one evening. Kristina had a very high fever and was quite sick. Her dad wanted her to take medicine, but she didn't want to take medicine.

I gave Kristina the microphone and asked her, "Would you like to share with everyone about how the Lord healed you?"

Kristina said, "I said to my papa, 'It's okay to go to the doctor, it's okay to take the pill, but that's not God's best.' Then I said to my papa, 'By God's stripes I am healed.'"

Of course, I reiterated that we thank God for doctors and nurses, but the truth is that Kristina didn't want to take the medication. While all this was going on, her mother was also praying in the Spirit. Her father was really concerned over Kristina because her temperature was rising to a dangerous level. But Kristina believed God would heal her.

Kristina's mother said that within a few minutes, her fever lifted off her and she slept through the night as though nothing had happened! God healed her.

I hope this story will build your faith, because the story goes on! Kristina's mother, Natasha, contacted me later, in August 2019, and gave me the following story:

On Tuesday, August 13, 2019, my husband was doing his physical training at work which involved placing weights on a sled and pushing it from one end to another several times. He had 700 pounds on his sled and upon turning his sled it went over his foot! He was in agony to say the least. It was a late work out so medical was closed so he had no choice but to wait until the next day. He came home literally hopping on one foot because it hurt terribly. He thought he broke his foot!

He sat down and I told Kristina to go lay hands on his foot and pray for healing. Before the night was over, he was walking normal. He acknowledged that he was healed! Glory to God!

The following day he went to work and the guys he works with were astonished at his quick recovery because they were with him when it happened! Glory to God!

My friend, aren't you encouraged to hear the testimony of the faith of a little child? It is God's will for you to be healed—and I can prove that from the Scriptures. You don't need a hundred Scriptures. You need one Scripture. One Scripture, when effectively planted in your heart and spoken through your mouth by faith, will yield all you need to overcome any sickness or disease.

First, pray about which Scripture God wants you to hang onto as you release your faith for your healing. The Lord talks to us all the time. You know He gives me Scriptures not only for healing, but for everything. As you read over the verses in this section, I believe the Holy Spirit will cause your heart to leap when there is a verse that is especially written for you, your circumstance, and your faith.

By whose stripes you were healed.

(1 Peter 2:24)

Praise the LORD, my soul,
   and never forget all the good he has done:
      He is the one who forgives all your sins,
         the one who heals all your diseases,
         the one who rescues your life from the pit,
         the one who crowns you with mercy and compassion,
         the one who fills your life with blessings
            so that you become young again like an eagle.

(Psalm 103:2–5 GW)

So then, since we have a great high priest who has entered heaven, Jesus the Son of God, let us hold firmly to what we believe. (Hebrews 4:14 NLT)

Beloved, I pray that you may prosper in all things and be in health, just as your soul prospers. (3 John 1:2)

That it might be fulfilled which was spoken by Isaiah the prophet, saying:

"He Himself took our infirmities
And bore our sicknesses."

(Matthew 8:17)

Did one or more of these verses ring true and speak to your heart? Hang onto that verse! Write this verse as a note to yourself on your cell phone! Place a hand-written note with this verse on it beside your bathroom mirror, kitchen sink, or on your car's dashboard. Pray it up to God, out loud, when you see it there each day.

Wayne contacted me not long ago and said that he was ill, and his kidneys were in "dire need of prayer." We prayed together and later praised God together for his healing. Wayne wrote to me and said:

Dear Pastor Jo,

I am happy to report that my kidney functions came back better than they have been in a long time! Thank you so much for your prayers and being a woman used by the Lord. I told several people about your ministry and I've been praying for God to enlarge your territory!

Thank you again,

Wayne

When God looks at you, He sees you as the healed of the Lord. The devil is the one that is lying to you. He is the one that is putting the symptoms on you, but when God looks on you, He doesn't see you as sick and He doesn't even see your sin. He sees you as the righteousness of God in Christ Jesus. When you were born again you became a brand new being, so your spirit is totally new, according to 2 Corinthians 5:17. You became a new creature or a brand-new species in Christ. A lot of people think it takes a lot of faith to be healed, but it doesn't take any more faith to be healed than it did for you to accept Jesus as your Lord and Savior. It's the same amount of faith. It's just believing.

Faith is not something that you do. Faith is a response to what God has already done on your behalf. Faith is simply acting like the Word of God is true. Friend, first you must believe that He wants you well. The Bible says it is by His stripes ye were healed, but first you are going to have to believe it. Matthew 9:35 says that Jesus went through all the towns and all the villages teaching in their synagogues, proclaiming the good news of the kingdom, and healing every disease and sickness. How many did He heal? It says that He healed *every* disease and *every* sickness.

First Peter 2:24 tells us that Jesus personally carried our sins in His body on the cross, so that we can be dead to sin and live for what is right—for by His wounds you are healed. For example, you are not going to be a saint, you already are a saint. That's right—you already are a saint! You know this is what's keeping so many people that are sick from receiving their healing? They open their mouth and instead of thanking God for their healing, they say, "I believe God is going to heal me. I believe that I am going to be healed." You are not going to be anything because you already are!

We need to understand that God's Word is just not mere letters on a page. His Word is alive with His spirit and His power. They are not just some words on a page. He says in John 6:63, "The words that I speak to you are spirit, and they are life." The strongest prayers that we can pray are the prayers full of the Word of God.

GOD, ARE YOU LISTENING?

Recently, I looked at my flower beds and our lawn and I noticed that they were not looking as healthy or as pretty as they normally do that time of the year. The grass had a lot of brown spots and my flowers were not as large or blooming. The rose bushes are normally covered in roses. Everybody else's roses were blooming and mine weren't doing anything. I realized that they had not been fed any nutrients for a long time and they needed to be fed. The people who had been doing our yard had not elected to feed everything, so my husband called the lawn people to come and put fertilizer down. At that time, the Lord revealed to me that this is what happens to our faith. When our faith is not being fed the Word of God, it becomes weak.

God's Word is food and medicine!

> My child, pay attention to what I say.
>> Listen carefully to my words.
> Don't lose sight of them.
>> Let them penetrate deep into your heart,
> for they bring life to those who find them,
>> and healing to the whole body.
>
> (Proverbs 4:20–22 NLT)

God's Word is medicine to all of your flesh, *to the whole body*. That is what God wants. He wants a whole and healthy body. You can't just hear the Word once a week and be well fed, no more than you can eat one meal a week and stay alive. Some people only hear the Word once a week and most of the time right after they hear the Word they go and feed on other things, things that counter the Word they just heard. Sometimes you can lose the Word you heard in the few minutes it takes you to leave the church and get to the parking lot. The devil can come and snatch it before you even get to your car sometimes.

I believe that God has given me enough Scriptures in this chapter that by the time you finish reading it, you will be convinced that God wants you healed. Romans 10:17 says that faith comes by hearing, and hearing by the Word of God.

A lot of people have asked me, "Pastor Jo, would you pray that I have more faith?"

I answer, "No, I can't do that. I can pray for you to be healed. I can pray for you to have a financial breakthrough. I can pray for reconciliation, but I can't pray for you to have more faith because faith comes from hearing!"

The only way you are going to get more faith is by hearing the Word of God, reading the Word of God, thinking about the Word of God, because that is what God said. Faith comes by hearing and hearing comes from the Word of God. The more you hear the Word, the more faith you are going to have. You see, God's Word is a lamp to our feet in a dark and fallen world. Without His Word we would have no way to even know God. Without the Word of God, we wouldn't even know how to do His will. We wouldn't know what His will is concerning our healing or anything else if we didn't have the Word.

Paul told the Thessalonians in 1 Thessalonians 2:13 that he was thankful the people in Thessalonica accepted the Word and that the Word "continues to work in you who believe" (NLT). Child of God, if you will take this Word as a Word from Paul it won't work for you. If you take this Word as a Word from Pastor Jo it won't work for you. But if you will take this Word as a Word from God it will work for you. Take this Word as if it is God Himself talking to you. If you will do this, then I can promise you that it will work. If you will take this Word as if it is God speaking to you (because truly it is) then His Word will work.

When you are speaking God's Word, it is Him talking to you. When you read the Bible, it is Him talking to you. That Word will push everything out of you that needs to be pushed out. Hallelujah! God said He is not a man that He should lie nor the Son of Man that He should have to repent or change His mind.

GOD, ARE YOU LISTENING?

I'm going to repeat myself, but I want to make sure you get this. If you will take the Scriptures on healing as a Word from God Himself for your situation, I can promise you that it will work for you. Please, don't pay any attention to this messenger, just focus on the Word and then I can promise you that it will work. I'm thankful that God never changes His mind. Has He ever spoken and failed to act? Has He ever promised and not carried it through? Never!

Jesus used many ways to heal the sick and the afflicted. One of the ways that He healed people was to lay hands on the sick. But another way to be healed is by the hearing of the Word of God.

Some people think that the only way that God heals is through manifestations of the gift of the Spirit, but we don't always have to wait for miraculous moving. All we have to do is hear the Word, believe the Word, and act on the Word. We have to act like God's Word is true.

You need to keep in mind that when the gifts of the Spirit are not in manifestation you can still be healed, as I said, through faith in God's Word.

Brother Kenneth Hagin flowed in the gift of healing, but he would always teach God's Word on healing for several nights at his meetings before he prayed for anybody. He taught them the Word of God about healing. Then when he did call people to the front for healing, he would ask them what Word, what Scripture, they were standing on. He would ask them what they were believing.

The Word of God is anointed, my friend, and God's Word is the same whether you or I feel the anointing or not. You don't always feel the anointing. People are so hung up on feelings that they miss out on a lot. You cannot let your feelings dictate to you what God has given to you. Let me also say that you don't have to have a feeling to experience the healing in your body. It's a big mistake to base your healing on a feeling. There again I'm going to repeat this. You don't have to feel healed in order to be healed.

PASTOR JOANNE RAMSAY

Brother Hagin is with the Lord now, but Pastor Sandra Kennedy from Augusta, Georgia, ministers under the healing anointing. She has a healing school and all they do all day long is teach God's Word to those that come for healing. People come from all over the world to this healing school. They see cancer healed. They see diabetes healed. They see new parts grow on people's bodies. They have seen people rise from the dead. What are they doing? Brothers and sisters, they are just ministering to them the Word of God. They even go into the hospitals and minister the Word of God. They speak to the people and they call them to live and command them to get up. The spirit can hear. The body may not hear at times, but that spirit can hear. So they talk to that person in the hospital. You may not think that person can hear you, but their spirit inside of them can hear. You talk to him and tell him to get out of that bed. Say, "You are healed in Jesus' name," and start quoting the Word to them. You know, that is better medicine than the hospital has. Their spirit can hear you. Why do I say that? Your spirit never dies. Your spirit is not in a coma.

In 2 Timothy 4, Paul told young Timothy to preach the Word. Why? The power and the anointing are in God's Word.

My husband David told me one night that as I was teaching the Word, his eye began to hurt him a lot. It grew worse and worse. He had recently had eye surgery and he said his eye was hurting him so badly that he thought he was going to have to get up and leave in the middle of the service.

David told me later, "All of a sudden, I thought to myself, I don't have to put up with this! The moment I thought that, I was healed before I even prayed."

Actually, what happened was that he believed in his heart that he didn't have to accept the pain and he received his healing by hearing the Word. He received his healing right then and there. I didn't even know about it. We pray for each other and pray for ourselves, but he didn't even tell me about that until much later.

GOD, ARE YOU LISTENING?

God gave you and me the power and wisdom to deal with whatever circumstances come along in life. You just have to believe that God has already released His power and made provision for you, even when there is no physical evidence to support that fact. This may surprise you, but most of the time there will not be any evidence at first that you have been healed.

Let me ask you a question. Did Jesus ever put sickness on anyone? Have you ever read in the Scriptures where Jesus put sickness on anyone? When people came to Jesus for healing, did He ever turn even one person away? Did He ever turn anybody away? No. He never turned anyone away, saying, "No, it's not my will to heal you." He never said, "Well, just suffer a little bit longer." He never told anybody that.

God calls sickness and disease satanic oppression. Satan is the author of sickness. Jesus is our healer. He is our deliverer through everything.

I remember several years ago that I couldn't even move my left arm. I don't even remember how it happened. I just woke up one morning and I couldn't even lift a glass of water and I couldn't stretch my arm out or lift it up. I laid my other hand on my arm and I prayed and began to speak to the muscles, joints, and nerves. I commanded them to line up with the Word of God. I called my arm healed in Jesus' name. Did the pain go away immediately? No, it did not. But I had a choice whether to believe what I was feeling or believe what God's Word said!

I chose to trust God's Word, even though there was no physical evidence that I was healed. The next time I prayed, I thanked God for healing my arm. I continued to thank Him for healthy joints, muscles and nerves. It got so difficult that the pain caused me to break out in a cold sweat sometimes. I had to sit up in bed to even turn over, and it was very painful. Even so, every day it would feel better and better, until one night about six months later I was invited to minister in this small town in North Carolina. As I sat there through the praise and worship, I was able to lift my right arm in praise, but not the left one. All of a sudden, it was kind of like the Lord tapped me on the shoulder and said, "Lift your arm." I did lift it all the way up, praise the Lord! Then I lifted both hands and praised God.

The question is this. Was I healed when I lifted my arm, or was I healed the day I laid hands on myself and prayed? I was healed the moment I prayed. Even though there was no evidence, I knew I was healed all that time. That is having faith and confidence in the unseen.

There are so many of God's children that are sick and suffering under the hands of Satan. According to His Word, God has made provision for you to be well, to be healed. I've been healed of many things since I became a Christian, and I'm sure that you have, too. Let me share with you another healing story.

Right after I accepted the Lord as my Savior back in 1992, I was diagnosed with two cysts on my ovaries and a growth on my lips. I had to postpone my surgery for the ovaries because I had a seminar coming up and I couldn't have the surgery at the time that the doctor wanted me to have the surgery. So when it came time for me to have the surgery, of course, I had to go back in and they did another ultrasound for the pre-op. The first time when they did the ultrasound, I had two cysts. When I went back to get the pre-op, they did another ultrasound and the doctors couldn't find anything. It was all gone. I was a new Christian then and I didn't have a lot of faith. I wasn't even sure about any of this stuff! So it wasn't left up to me. It is never left up to us. Thank God it's not left up to us. He just wants us to have faith!

The hospital had given me two photos—one photo of the ultrasound the first time they took it, with two cysts. The second photo was from the second ultrasound and there were no cysts. Like I said, I was a baby Christian and I put those photos up on my refrigerator and kept them there for a long time. That was my testimony! I had one photo with cysts and one without cysts and I thought it was awesome!

Shortly after that, I was washing my face one night and a growth fell off my mouth and fell in the sink. Hallelujah! It just fell off into the sink.

I went running to my husband and I said, "Look! It's gone!"

He said, "What happened?"

I said, "I don't know. I was washing my face and it just fell off into the sink!"

Hallelujah! Now, I was a new Christian, so I had not had time to build up a lot of faith. According to the Bible, it is God's will to heal and to heal everyone. Acts 10:38 says that God anointed Jesus of Nazareth with the Holy Ghost and with the power and He went about doing good and healing all that were oppressed of the devil.

You might wonder, why don't the things that God has already put in our spirit manifest automatically? Why do I have to do something to receive from God? You know, everything that God has made available comes through the Spirit. That is true, whether or not it comes out of your spirit and into the physical realm where you can see it. It isn't dependent upon God, it's dependent upon whether or not you believe that God has already done it. Faith works by simply acknowledging, or getting a revelation of, what is already in you (Philemon 1:6).

You see, our faith is the conduit through which God's power flows into our lives. Let me pause a minute here and define a conduit. A *conduit* is a natural or artificial channel or passage through which something is transferred or delivered to another person. Another meaning of *conduit* is a means of bearing or transporting. And that is how our faith causes what God has for us to be transferred or delivered from the spiritual realm to the natural realm. Faith is the conduit through which God's power flows into our lives.

Zachariah 4:6 says it is not by my power, but God's Spirit. It is by the Spirit of God that you are going to get healed and through your belief in the power of the Spirit of God. First Thessalonians 1:5 says, "For our gospel did not come to you in word only, but also in power and in the Holy Spirit." First Corinthians 4:20 (NLT) says, "For the Kingdom of God is not just a lot of talk; it is living by God's power."

Let me pray with you right now:

Father in heaven, I thank You for all of Your promises in the Bible. I thank You for Your presence. I thank You, Holy Spirit, for Your presence that flows right now into Your child as we say this prayer together. I thank You, Jesus, that You have given us permission to use Your name, and that at the name of Jesus every knee must bow in heaven, on earth, and under the earth.

Right now, I command sickness to bow its knee. I command every demonic force to bow its knee in the name of Jesus. Father, I thank You that You are working through me, doing mighty works, and for the Holy Spirit, who is here with me to help me.

I thank You for raising my faith to a higher level as I read this chapter on Your healing power. You are renewing my mind and I praise You!

Father, I thank You for healing me. Your Word says in Matthew 8:17 that You took my infirmities and bore my sickness. I realize that Satan is the oppressor. He is the one that came to kill and destroy me. But I believe that as it says in Acts 10:38 that You anointed Jesus of Nazareth with the Holy Ghost and with power and He went about doing good and healing all those who were oppressed by the devil. That includes me. Jesus, You are my deliverer. It says in First Peter 2:24 that by Jesus' stripes on His back I am healed. Hallelujah! I believe You said it, and I believe Your Word, Lord. Father, again I give You all the praise and glory in advance for all that You are about to do. In Jesus' name, Amen. Hallelujah!

—⁓—

CHAPTER 5

Believing God for a Baby

For this child I prayed, and the Lord has granted me my petition which I asked of Him.

First Samuel 1:27

God gives us promises in His Word regarding our offspring. David wrote in Psalm 113:9 that God makes the barren woman to keep house, and to be a joyful mother of children. That's a powerful promise! Sometimes our faith is tested when months or even years go by without seeing that promise fulfilled. Don't give up!

Some parents are concerned about carrying a child to full term. One of the blessings that God gives to His children is to carry their young to full term: "No one shall suffer miscarriage or be barren in your land; I will fulfill the number of your days" (Exodus 23:26).

In fact, David writes in Psalm 139 that God formed each baby in the womb of their mother:

For You formed my inward parts;
You covered me in my mother's womb.
I will praise You, for I am fearfully and wonderfully made;

GOD, ARE YOU LISTENING?

Marvelous are Your works,
And that my soul knows very well.
My frame was not hidden from You,
When I was made in secret,
And skillfully wrought in the lowest parts of the earth.
Your eyes saw my substance, being yet unformed.
And in Your book they all were written,
The days fashioned for me,
When as yet there were none of them.

(Psalm 139:14–16)

Do you see the power of God that shapes and molds a child in the womb?

When we share testimonies with one another, it builds our faith. Before I go further in sharing a Bible story about conception, I would like to share a more recent testimony with you from a young woman named Felicia:

Hi Pastor Ramsay,

I have always loved the Lord, but never truly called on Him. My husband and I had trouble conceiving and I couldn't understand why. I was upset, mad, angry, and full of despair. I met a lot of people who loved the Lord and gave me God's Word, and then I met you. You know that I always tell you that you have a phone line straight to God. You saw my pain and despair. You took my hand at a meeting and said, "You can either speak life or you can speak death."

I will never forget that.

Felicia

Later on, Felicia sent me this email:

PASTOR JOANNE RAMSAY

Dear Pastor Ramsay,

Thank you for going BOLDLY to the throne of God and praying over me. You equipped me with many verses from the Bible that I needed in order to fight the enemy. You helped me to expect a child through this verse: "'For I know the plans I have for you,' declares the LORD, 'plans to prosper you and not to harm you, plans to give you hope and a future'" (Jeremiah 29:11 NIV).

Pastor Ramsay, you taught me that God would give me the desires of my heart. I believed God. I want you to know that you were right! My beautiful son Grant Dominick was born, healthy and strong! Now I've learned to always lean on God, to ask Him and to believe. Praise God!

Felicia

There is power in a testimony like that! God wants to bless you, but we can grow quite a bit through the struggle, too.

Perhaps you or someone you know can identify with the wide range of emotions that a woman experiences when she is having difficulty conceiving a child. That inner struggle reminds us of a woman in the Bible named Hannah. What made Hannah's situation especially painful is that Hannah was teased by other family members because she was barren. Hannah was a wise woman. She came to the right place. She went to God's Word and to God's house to get her answers.

So Peninnah would taunt Hannah and make fun of her because the LORD had kept her from having children. Year after year it was the same—Peninnah would taunt Hannah as they went to the Tabernacle. Each time, Hannah would be reduced to tears and would not even eat.

"Why are you crying, Hannah?" Elkanah would ask. "Why aren't you eating? Why be downhearted just because you have no

children? You have me—isn't that better than having ten sons?"
(1 Samuel 1:6–8 NLT)

Hannah's husband Elkanah found out quickly that having a husband was *not* the same thing as having ten sons! God put it within a woman's heart to nurture life. If you put a little boy and a little girl into the same room full of toys, the boy will likely pick up a truck or a power action figure. A little girl will pick up a doll and cuddle it, wrap it in a blanket, and pretend to be a mother. Even single women gravitate to nurturing life through helping people in trouble, tending plants, or helping other family members with their children. Hannah was no different. She wanted a child more than anything else in the world.

What could Hannah do? She could pray and believe God for a child. I'm so glad that the Bible tells us what Hannah prayed, aren't you? Let's take a peek at how Hannah prayed after a worship service at the tabernacle in Jerusalem:

Once after a sacrificial meal at Shiloh, Hannah got up and went to pray. Eli the priest was sitting at his customary place beside the entrance of the Tabernacle. Hannah was in deep anguish, crying bitterly as she prayed to the LORD. And she made this vow: "O LORD of Heaven's Armies, if you will look upon my sorrow and answer my prayer and give me a son, then I will give him back to you. He will be yours for his entire lifetime, and as a sign that he has been dedicated to the LORD, his hair will never be cut."

As she was praying to the LORD, Eli watched her. Seeing her lips moving but hearing no sound, he thought she had been drinking. "Must you come here drunk?" he demanded. "Throw away your wine!"

"Oh no, sir!" she replied. "I haven't been drinking wine or anything stronger. But I am very discouraged, and I was pouring out my heart to the LORD. Don't think I am a wicked woman! For I have been praying out of great anguish and sorrow."

"In that case," Eli said, "go in peace! May the God of Israel grant the request you have asked of him."

"Oh, thank you, sir!" she exclaimed. Then she went back and began to eat again, and she was no longer sad. (1 Samuel 1:9–18 NLT)

You know, you have to feel sorry for Hannah in a way. She was teased by Peninnah at home and then, even when she called out to God at the temple, she was misunderstood and accused of being drunk! Wisely, Hannah did not take offense. She pressed in and told the priest, Eli, that she was praying in anguish and sorrow. Up until this time, Hannah was in tears and couldn't eat because she was so upset. In the end, she took her tears to God.

As soon as Eli said, "Go in peace! May the God of Israel grant the request you have asked of him," Hannah believed God. How do we know she believed God? We know that Hannah believed because she was no longer sad, and she began to eat again. The sorrow that had gripped her was gone, because Hannah believed that God would grant her a child! She had not yet conceived a child in her body, but faith was conceived in her heart! A seed of faith dropped into Hannah's heart and she knew that she was going to have a child!

We can see from this story that no one really understood how Hannah felt except God. Hannah didn't listen to what other people thought about her or her situation. She went to God and poured out her heart. Again, I want you to notice something. As soon as Eli said, "May God grant your request," she knew God heard her and believed that He would indeed answer her prayers for a child. Look what happened next: "And in due time she gave birth to a son. She named him Samuel, for she said, 'I asked the LORD for him'" (1 Samuel 1:20 NLT).

Oh, what joy filled her soul!

I'd like to tell you a true story about a dad who did not believe God would answer his prayers for a child. God had to shut his mouth before he totally ruined everything that God wanted to do for him! Let's look at this story:

> But the angel said to him, "Do not be afraid, Zacharias, for your prayer is heard; and your wife Elizabeth will bear you a son, and you shall call his name John. And you will have joy and gladness, and many will rejoice at his birth. For he will be great in the sight of the Lord." (Luke 1:13–15a)

Zacharias should have been jumping up and down for joy! Instead, he expressed doubt. Let's see how God responded to this daddy's doubt:

> And Zacharias said to the angel, "How shall I know this? For I am an old man, and my wife is well advanced in years."
>
> And the angel answered and said to him, "I am Gabriel, who stands in the presence of God, and was sent to speak to you and bring you these glad tidings. But behold, *you will be mute and not able to speak until the day these things take place, because you did not believe my words which will be fulfilled in their own time.*"
>
> And the people waited for Zacharias, and marveled that he lingered so long in the temple. But when he came out, he could not speak to them; and they perceived that he had seen a vision in the temple, for he beckoned to them and remained speechless. (Luke 1:18–22)

May I suggest to you that God had to shut this man's mouth so he would not express doubt and ruin all of God's plans? Whether God's plan for us is to adopt a child or conceive a child, we are required to proceed with God's plan by faith. You know from reading previous chapters that faith comes by hearing God's Word. God requires us to declare His Word as the only truth in a matter.

Six months after Elizabeth conceived her baby John, the angel Gabriel visited earth again to deliver a message from God. Gabriel came to Mary, a virgin, and told her she would have a son, God's Son, by the Holy Spirit. Gabriel said, "For with God, nothing shall be impossible."

How did Mary respond when Gabriel announced that she would carry the Son of God, conceived by the Holy Ghost? Mary's faith is astounding! Look at her response: "Then Mary said, 'Behold the maidservant of the Lord! Let it be to me according to your word'" (Luke 1:38).

Glory to God! Do you hear this woman's faith? This time Gabriel did not have to deliver a rebuke. He did not have to mute Mary's mouth. In fact, when she visited her cousin Elizabeth later on, Mary broke into a song of rejoicing!

And Mary said:

"My soul magnifies the Lord,
And my spirit has rejoiced in God my Savior.
For He has regarded the lowly state of His maidservant;
For behold, henceforth all generations will call me blessed.
For He who is mighty has done great things for me,
And holy is His name.
And His mercy is on those who fear Him
From generation to generation."

(Luke 1:46–50)

My friend, I pray that one of these testimonies and one of these Scriptures leap out at you and grab your heart! May the Word of God be planted within you like a seed and your miracle child be in your arms on the given day that God decides! "He gives the childless woman a family, / making her a happy mother. / Praise the Lord!" (Psalm 113:9 NLT).

My friend Hope tells me the story of how God granted her a child. For years she wanted a child and prayed for one. When Hope was thirty-two years old, she read a Scripture that someone wrote in a magazine article. The article wasn't about children, but that Scripture came alive inside of her when she read it! She read about childless Abraham and Sarah from the book of Romans:

> In hope against hope he [Abraham] believed, so that he might become a father of many nations according to that which had been spoken, "So shall your descendants be." Without becoming weak in faith he contemplated his own body, now as good as dead since he was about a hundred years old, and the deadness of Sarah's womb; yet, with respect to the promise of God, he did not waver in unbelief but grew strong in faith, giving glory to God, and being fully assured that what God had promised, He was able also to perform. (Romans 4:18–21 NASB)

Of course, Hope's name was in there so that verse stood out to her, that in hope against hope, Abraham believed God. Hope believed and did not waver in unbelief but grew strong in faith. The Word of God in Romans 4:18–21 became more than just words on paper. Chapter 4 of Romans became a seed of faith dropped into her heart. Hope said,

> From that day on, I was no longer sad. I couldn't explain it, but I knew deep inside that I would have a child. I carefully chose two friends that I would tell, two friends who had previously prayed for me to conceive. Right away one said she saw that twinkle in my eye and she knew that I was truly in faith and I would conceive. The next year, I delivered a baby boy and we named him Johnathan, which means *gift from God*.

> One of my favorite verses in the Bible is Jeremiah 29:11 (NIV): "'For I know the plans I have for you,' declares the LORD, 'plans to prosper you and not to harm you, plans to give you hope and a future.'"

Sometimes God's best plan points a parent to adoption. One of my listeners wrote in just recently that after falling forty feet down a mountain, she was told she would never be able to walk or to have children. She emailed me with this report:

Dearest Pastor Jo Anne, my God, my precious Abba, blessed me to walk! I can move and God blessed us with two children though adoption! I believe in God, absolutely, without a shred of doubt. My God is great and can do all things.

Hallelujah! God always has a plan. My niece prayed for children and, of course, I prayed for her to have children as well. I asked her if she would share a little bit of her story in my book because if you have ever been through infertility, you know the anguish of heart that it can cause. I've asked Karen to tell you her story in her own words:

My husband and I tried for three and a half years to conceive. We did infertility drugs. We did every avenue available, except in-vitro fertilization (IVF). For some reason, I had a personal conviction not to do IVF. I just never had peace about that for us. I never felt that was the route God was going to use to give us the child we were praying for.

There were tears and times we felt discouraged. I met with my Aunt Jo and we prayed in her kitchen. Aunt Jo said that it's not because of anointing oil, but it's God—the great physician and I AM WHO I AM. (A lady in the church had anointed me with oil and told me to anoint my stomach every day with oil.) So, when Aunt Jo came to pray for me, she said the Lord impressed her *not* to use the oil. I began to cry. I just wanted the Lord to touch me. Aunt Jo said that God wanted me to know that He is almighty, and that's where the power comes from, not from using oil, or fertility drugs, or whatever.

GOD, ARE YOU LISTENING?

Time went on and we kept praying. The more we prayed, the more often God put things in front of us about adoption. Things were just in front of us all the time about adoption. We went to an informational meeting one night and we left there wanting to adopt. God did a huge transformation and changed our hearts to make us open to adoption. That process took about a year. Adoption has its ups and downs, like anything. We had an open adoption, and it's such a beautiful story!

The first time I met my son's biological mother, she looked at me and said, "This is your baby." I wondered, *how could she say that?* But God is good, and I believe He was working through her to look at me and say that. That was so selfless. She was more concerned about the health and well-being of the baby than of herself. That says a lot for the biological mother.

Then, when my adopted son Grady was four months old, I found out I was pregnant with my own biological baby! When we chose adoption, I felt like God had answered my prayer and He made me completely okay with being just an adoptive mom. So, when I found out I was pregnant with Jax, I was confused. He had made me so completely satisfied with being an adoptive mom. I didn't understand. I thought, *why this?* But now I do understand.

Grady and Jax are now thirteen months apart. Ultimately, God has the final say. I feel like God wanted Grady to come first. He had a reason for him to be in our family. Jax needed to be in our life. Grady needed to be in our life. I feel God has blessed us. God is good and He has the final say. He writes a much better story than we can write for ourselves. That's our story in a nutshell— but there were lot of tears and heartache along the way.

I hope that Karen's story has helped someone reading this book. She now has two sons a year apart. She got pregnant almost immediately after she adopted her first son! Glory to God!

It could be that you are trying to have a baby, but maybe the Lord is speaking to you about adoption. Sometimes parents can have their minds so set on having a biological baby that they won't consider adopting a child. As it turned out, Karen and her husband became focused on adoption and now they have two! It's really a double miracle. And God saw that precious young girl who was pregnant and crying out for a good mother for Grady. God sees everything.

You know, Romans 8:15 says that as God's children we receive a spirit of adoption and as His children we cry out to Him, "Abba! Father!" or, "Daddy! Father!" No one understands the joys of adoption like our God. I believe that God appointed extraordinary moms and dads to parent a child that they've carried in their heart, but not their bodies. This is a gift from God, just as Johnathan was a gift from God to Hope.

God wants a big family! He is delighted to give you a child to raise! Let's pray together right now for your child.

Father in Heaven, I know that You have loved us with an everlasting love. You sent Jesus, Your only Son, to give up His life so that You could have many sons and daughters. Thank You for adopting us! Thank You for loving us! We are thrilled to know that You will finally have Your family that has been the dream of Your heart since You created Adam and Eve.

"For this reason I bow my knees to the Father of our Lord Jesus Christ, from whom the whole family in heaven and earth is named, that He would grant you, according to the riches of His glory, to be strengthened with might through His Spirit in the inner man" (Ephesians 3:14–16). Father, I thank You that according to Your Word, many are the promises of God, and they all find their answer in Christ. Father, Your Word tells me to put You in remembrance of Your Word (Isaiah 43:26). I am so glad that Your Word says, "No one shall suffer miscarriage or be barren in your land; I will fulfill the number of your days" (Exodus 23:26).

GOD, ARE YOU LISTENING?

You said, Lord, that You make the barren woman to keep house, and to be a joyful mother of children (Psalm 113:9 KJV). So, Lord, based on Your Word, I am asking You to open my womb and fill it with life. I ask that as You were with Hannah, so You shall also be with me. As she found favor in Your sight, so I pray You will show me favor, too, by opening up my womb (1 Samuel 1:17–18).

Lord, You said to delight ourselves in the Lord, and You would give us the desires of our hearts (Psalm 37:4). Father, I desire to be a mother. I pray that as You blessed both Hannah and Elizabeth by opening up their wombs, that You will bless me by opening up my womb (Luke 1:36). Father, I know that nothing is impossible with You. To the one who believes, nothing is impossible. And I believe that You are opening up my womb even as I speak. So I thank You now in advance for showing me Your mercy and Your grace. In Jesus' name I pray. Amen.

—ɯ—

Chapter 6

When I Am Afraid

But when I am afraid, I will trust in You. I praise God for what he has promised. I trust in God, so why should I be afraid? What can mere mortals do to me?

Psalm 56:3–4 NLT

For God has not given us a spirit of fear, but of power and of love and of a sound mind.

Second Timothy 1:7

Research shows that many mental and physical illnesses come from our thought life rather than the surrounding environment or family genes. An undisciplined mind is filled with a continuous stream of worries and fears.

Does God want us to worry? No. Our bodies and our minds are not created to handle a multitude of concerns. Worry distresses our physical and mental systems. We can get pains, palpitations, and problems in our physical body and mind when we cave in to fear of our future.

The importance of capturing our fearful thoughts cannot be overstated. God wants to prepare us mentally, spiritually, and physically for the days ahead. Luke 21:26 tells us that in the last days circumstances around us are going to get worse, not better, and people's hearts will fail them because of fear.

> And there will be signs in the sun, in the moon, and in the stars; and on the earth distress of nations, with perplexity, the sea and the waves roaring; *men's hearts failing them from fear and the expectation of those things which are coming on the earth*, for the powers of the heavens will be shaken. (Luke 21:25, 26)

If we truly believe that Jesus is coming again and believe what the Bible says in Luke 21, then we need to prepare our hearts right now how to respond to these distresses and perplexities without fear. We want to be mature, and help people come to know Christ and be saved from sin before Jesus returns.

That's why the Bible says emphatically that God has not given us a spirit of fear. Fear is not from God. Sadly, if we do not pray God's Word over our fears, we may find our lives a cycle where we wake up worrying and we go to bed worrying.

There are a few verses that send fear away from us, but the one I repeat most often in prayer and thanks to God is this one: "For God has not given us a spirit of fear, but of power and of love and of a sound mind" (2 Timothy 1:7). When I feel the power of fear sneaking up on me or if I suddenly realize that I'm tempted to rehearse fearful thoughts, I pray this verse back to the Lord. I say,

> *Lord God, I thank You that this spirit of fear is not from You. For You did not give me a spirit of fear, but of power, and love, and a sound mind. Thank You, Lord.*
>
> *Spirit of fear, I take authority over you; I bind you up and command you to flee my mind now, in the name of Jesus.*

This is prayer in action! And when I speak the Word from 2 Timothy 1:7 and Luke 10:19, the thoughts disappear. The devil cowers. All plans devised by the enemy against me are thwarted because I refuse to listen to them! If fear persists or returns again, then you grab another believer in Christ and ask them to agree with you concerning whatever fear is trying to torment you. Agree together that fearful thoughts are cast down, away from your mind altogether.

As a child of God, there is no need to ever be fearful. I realize that we are tempted on a daily basis to fear everything. There is so much going on in the world today and danger on every side, but our Father reassures us that we need not be afraid. Isaiah 41:10 says, "Don't be afraid, for I am with you. / Don't be discouraged, for I am your God. / I will strengthen you and help you. / I will hold you up with My victorious right hand." Hallelujah!

God said you will look in vain for those who tried to conquer you, but they will come to nothing. For the Lord your God will hold you by your right hand. And He says to His little ones, "Don't be afraid." Amen.

You may not realize this, but worrying is a sin, because when you're worrying all you're saying is, *I'm not trusting God*. God knows that fearful things are going to happen on this earth. However, King David writes that he was able to trust God *when* he was afraid: "Whenever I am afraid, I will trust in You" (Psalm 56:3).

Notice that David didn't write that he was never afraid. No, David said, "*When* I am afraid, I will trust in You." We all see fearful things whether on the news or in real life. Each one of us has experienced one fearful thing or another. What I'm saying is, don't try to handle the situation yourself instead of trusting God with it. Worry is a sin. God wants to deliver us from all our fears. Look what Jesus said:

Therefore do not worry, saying, "What shall we eat?" or "What shall we drink?" or "What shall we wear?" For after all these things the Gentiles seek. For your heavenly Father knows that you need all these things. But seek first the kingdom of God and His righteousness, and all these things shall be added to you. Therefore do not worry about tomorrow, for tomorrow will worry about its own things. Sufficient for the day is its own trouble.

(Matthew 6:31–34)

Even though we may know the Word of God says not to worry, the temptation can be there. Some people fear the unknown. There may be no cause to worry at all, but vain and fearful imaginations can march through our minds and creep into our thought life.

Other fears are not from our imaginations, but haunt us due to a fearful experience in the past. Many combat veterans deal with post-traumatic stress syndrome, or PTSD. But combat veterans aren't the only ones who deal with this. If we experience or witness a natural disaster, a serious accident, an embarrassment, a feeling of inadequacy, an act of violence, or a host of other fearful things, we can feel shell-shocked. The fear of that event repeating itself can loom large. Sometimes the words that someone said to us replay in our minds and try to paralyze us. If we recall or entertain that fear day after day, the fear will grow and enlarge itself. Anxiety and flashbacks can bring that bad memory to the forefront and cause intense physical and emotional reactions.

I'm no different than anyone else. Recently, I experienced a traumatic event. I had two choices, just like you: to allow fear to take over; or to face my fears, pray over my fears, and discipline my thoughts.

Just a few months ago, I was working out at the health club. My husband and I go to the health club most mornings to work out because, like you, we want to stay healthy. I always take my cell phone with me so I can listen to praise and worship while I'm on the treadmill. This particular morning, as I was about to step onto the treadmill, I was looking at my phone. I wasn't paying attention to the treadmill.

I hadn't noticed that the person before me had left the treadmill running, so when I went to step on it, it just flipped me up. It was horrific! I can't tell you how horrible it was. It flipped me from one side to the other, threw me up in the air, back down onto the treadmill, and finally like a bag of potatoes, tossed me on the floor.

The accident bruised the ribs on my left side, busted up the side of my face, and damaged my leg quite a bit. I was in so much pain, I was in tears. They called an ambulance to come for me. I was terrified!

They checked me over and found out the ribs were just bruised. Of course, when you have bruised ribs, there's not much you can do other than wait for them to heal. So I came back home and was laid up for a while. I did what the doctor told me to do. It was about two months before I was able to go back to the health club. I was tempted not to go back because, like most people would be, I was fearful.

Finally, I decided that my fear was not going to get the best of me. I went back to the health club and tried to get on the treadmill, but I found that I couldn't get on by myself. So my husband took me by the hand and helped me onto the treadmill. I turned it on—going very, very slow.

My husband encouraged me, and said, "We can stay as long as you're able to stay. If you want to get off, just let me know and we'll get off."

I turned on my praise and worship music, like I normally do, and then I began to pray. I spoke God's word over my body and I declared out loud, *"Lord, I thank You that You did not give me a spirit of fear, but of power, love, and a sound mind. I thank You, Lord, that I shall not be afraid, for You said You are always with me, so I don't have to be afraid. So, Lord, I thank You for giving me strength and courage to get back up on this treadmill and face it."*

I only walked on the treadmill for a few minutes that day. My husband took me by the hand when I told him I was ready, and I got back off. The next day I went back, and it was the same thing—my husband took me by the hand and led me back up on the treadmill again.

We did this for a few days, but after that I was able to get up on the treadmill by myself without any help. Before you know it, I was back at full speed again. But I can tell you that, from that point on, I never stepped back up on the treadmill without first looking to see if it was on!

Each one of us has experienced fearful things, but praying God's Word over that anxiety will bring us to victory every time! I thank God every day for the power that is in the spoken Word of God and how we can take His Word, the Word that has all power, and speak it over our situations, no matter what they are—fear, health, whatever it is. As I go to step up on the treadmill or do anything else I might be fearful about, I just repeat what the Lord says: *"Lord, I thank You that You did not give me a spirit of fear, but You gave me a spirit of power, love, and a sound mind. Thank You, Lord."*

God's Word works. It worked for me, and it will work for you, too. You just have to come face to face with those giants sometimes, and you have to stand strong—you have to do it like David, "when you are afraid," in other words. You can do it. I know you can. If I can do it, you can do it!

It can be difficult to recover from a terrifying event. One of the strongest temptations we encounter is the fear that something bad, something that happened in the past, will return and repeat itself. That's a lie. You have to cast that thought down. Just because something bad happened the last time I was in the health club doesn't mean that every time I go there I'm going to experience pain and trauma. I prayed and I spoke the Word of God in order to combat the anxiety. Frankly, I had to stand against fear, even when I was afraid!

Like David, I had to say, "Lord, I'm feeling anxious right now. But even when I am afraid, I will trust in You."

There's an old saying in cowboy country that if you're thrown off a horse, you get back up and ride that horse again, right away! After my body physically recovered so that I could begin to exercise again, I determined that I would "get back on the horse." My husband, David, went back with me to that health club. He held my hand when I got back on the treadmill. He knew it wasn't easy for me to go back there.

I want to encourage you, whatever worry is rattling you, to face your fear. I got back up on that treadmill. Was I afraid? I admit, I was afraid. So I tell people, "Do it afraid!" In other words, dear saint, do what God asks you to do even when you are afraid. You just have to continue to trust Him.

Am I afraid now? No, I'm not afraid anymore. I am more cautious when I get on and off the treadmill, or any other health club equipment. I keep an eye on what's going on around me, but my heart is not racing; my mind is not rehearsing that traumatic accident morning, noon, and night. When the devil brings the memory back to my mind as I go to step up on the treadmill, I just repeat what the Lord says. *"Lord, I thank You that You did not give me a spirit of fear, but You gave me a spirit of power, love, and a sound mind."*

We have to be careful what we allow ourselves to think about. If we feed on the Word of God, then our hearts will be thinking about the Word of God. Proverbs 23:7 says that as a man thinks in his heart, so is he. In Luke 5:22, Jesus perceived his disciples' thoughts and said to them, "Why are you reasoning in your hearts?" Jesus noticed that they were reasoning in their hearts when he was talking to them.

According to researchers, a whopping 75% to 98% of illnesses that plague us today are a direct result of our thought life. Only 13% are attributed to our diet, genetics, and environment. I want you to think about that. Those are some high numbers. Research shows that 75% to 95% of doctor visits are stress-related ailments. Think about that. I'm telling you these things because you can have control. You have control over that stress, over that anxious feeling, over a panic attack, and over those sicknesses that are attacking your body. They are coming from anxious thoughts and fears.

Your thoughts are powerful!

Did you ever pray about something and later find yourself thinking a negative thought about that situation you were just praying for? That's a common experience to most of us, I think. But you know, God designed us humans with the capability to observe our own thoughts.

GOD, ARE YOU LISTENING?

If you are struggling with a fearful thought, there is hope! If we find ourselves thinking a harmful or tormenting thought, God's Word says that we can get rid of that bad thought:

> Casting down arguments and every high thing that exalts itself against the knowledge of God, bringing every thought into captivity to the obedience of Christ. (2 Corinthians 10:5)

This Scripture is showing us that it is possible to:
1. Realize we are thinking the wrong thing;
2. Catch that wrong thought;
3. Cast that thought down.

You are completely capable through Jesus Christ! Throw down the anxious, fearful, or lustful thought and teach yourself to say what God says. Another translation (VOICE) puts it this way: "We are taking prisoners of every thought, every emotion, and subduing them into obedience to the Anointed One." *Subdue* means to overpower by superior force; to conquer, to bring into subjection. My friend, *we are that superior force,* because we have the whole Godhead living inside us. We are that superior force that's going to capture those thoughts and subdue them and bring them in.

Are you ready to pray? Let's do this!

Lord, I thank You that I am not moved by what I feel and what I see. I am only moved by what the Word of God says. The Word of God says that You have given me the power to speak to any situation, even the ones that scare me. I declare that when I am afraid, I will trust in You. I thank You, Lord, for the power to face my fear and "do it afraid."

PASTOR JOANNE RAMSAY

Lord, I thank You that You did not give me a spirit of fear, but You gave me a spirit of power, love, and a sound mind. I refuse to worry about my tomorrows, because You said that tomorrow will take care of itself. Even in the shadows of death's darkness, I am not overcome with fear, because You are with me in my trials. You are with me in those dark moments and Your protection and guidance give me comfort.

I pray, Lord, that You will give me the grace to monitor the words coming from my lips that I may not speak words of fear, doubt and unbelief. Father, with Your help, I purpose to speak what You say about my situations. And when I am afraid, I will put my trust in You. In Jesus' name, Amen.

—⁓—

CHAPTER 7

Battle the Bully—Satan

Behold, I give unto you power to tread on serpents and scorpions, and over all the power of the enemy: and nothing shall by any means hurt you.

Luke 10:19 KJV

Are you hurting today? Do you feel alone? Perhaps you feel like the devil is beating you up lately. So many of God's children are hurting these days. They are burdened down with yokes of bondage and sicknesses in their bodies, or they lack the finances to take care of their needs, but as God's children we have to stand our ground. We can stand firm and battle the devil through the power of God's Word. You and I have to tell Satan:

- You're not going to have my health!
- You're not going to have my mind!
- You're not going to have my child!
- You're not going to have my job!
- You're not going to have my family!
- I belong to God. I am blood-bought and paid for and I'll fight you with every fiber of my being.
- I am not alone! God is with me!

- You will not get the last word. I'll fight you, Devil, 'til I die!
- Hallelujah! Praise God!

Before we go too far into our battle against the bully, the devil, I want to remind you that your tongue has already chosen which side you're on—God's side or the devil's side. You can either say what God's Word says about a situation or you can choose to say what Satan says about your circumstances. Have you been on the devil's side lately? Well, take the opportunity right now to stop agreeing with the devil's sickness, poverty, and death, and take sides with God and His Word!

I believe in putting on the armor of God and taking authority over the evil one, but first you have to get your own words under control. James 3:6 says that the tongue is a *blazing* fire and it seeks to ignite an entire world of vices. Look at this familiar Scripture in James from THE VOICE translation:

> We all stumble along the way. If a person never speaks hurtful words or shouts in anger or profanity, then he has achieved perfection. The one who can control his tongue can also control the rest of his body. It's like when we place a metal bit into a horse's mouth to ride it; we can control its entire body with the slightest movement of our hands. Have you ever seen a massive ship sailing effortlessly across the water? Despite its immense size and the fact that it is propelled by mighty winds, a small rudder directs the ship in any direction the pilot chooses. It's just the same with our tongues! It's a small muscle, capable of marvelous undertakings.
>
> And do you know how many forest fires begin with a single ember from a small campfire? The tongue is a blazing fire seeking to ignite an entire world of vices. The tongue is unique among all parts of the body because it is capable of corrupting the whole body. If that were not enough, it ignites and consumes

the course of creation with a fuel that originates in hell itself. (James 3:2–6 VOICE)

The tongue is unique among all parts of the body because it is capable of corrupting the whole body. When we do battle with the bully, Satan, we have to use our tongue. The trouble is that some people engage in self-destruction when they open their mouths and agree with the devil. You have to be careful that you don't "shoot yourself in the foot" while you're trying to do battle with the devil!

Let me be a bit more practical here so you don't miss what I'm trying to say. I want you to know that everyone hears you talk about your lack. The devil hears you talk about your lack. Your neighbors hear you talk about your lack. Your coworkers hear you talk about your lack. They hear you talk about your sickness. They hear you talking death. When you're speaking death, lack, sickness, or defeat, everybody hears you. Satan hears you. Your neighbors hear you. Maybe you've never given a lot of thought to this, but when you speak lack, it actually *stops* your finances. When you speak sickness, it actually *stops* your healing. The devil didn't have to do a thing except tempt you to open your mouth and deny God's healing, provision, victory, and life!

So the first rule of doing battle against the bully is to watch your tongue! Don't give the devil weapons to use against you. Shut your mouth unless God's Word is coming out. The authority of God increases in your life when you decide to live like this.

Ephesians 1 says that God raised Jesus up from the dead and then seated Him at God's right hand in the heavenly places, far above all principality and power and might and dominion, and every name that is named, not only in this age but also in that which is to come.

I was brushing my teeth one morning and God showed me a picture. Then He said, "I want you to draw me a picture of the three chairs." I knew what He meant. So I drew stick figures on chairs to show the Father, the Son, and me seated right beside them! The Holy Ghost is on the earth, my friend—you and I are sitting in heavenly places. We don't act like it sometimes, but God says that we are seated with Him far above the principalities and the darkness of this world.

God wants to give you a vision of where you are seated—that's where your authority is located, right beside Him. He didn't even ask you. He just made you sit down with Him when you accepted Jesus as Lord and Savior. Hallelujah! Look what Jesus said: "Behold, I give unto you power to tread on serpents and scorpions, and over all the power of the enemy: and nothing shall by any means hurt you" (Luke 10:19 KJV).

1. You have power to tread upon, which means to trample on, press, crush or injure something; in this case, the devil himself. It means to treat with disdainful harshness or cruelty. In other words, you have to stop being so nice to the devil. You can't keep saying, "Dear devil, would you just please leave me alone? Lord, I just wish the devil would leave me alone today. Lord, I just wish you would get this devil off my back." And God is saying, "You let him get on you, you get him off." God will get him off, but you've got to use the Word.

2. You've been given the power to speak to any situation. You can speak to those dry bones or anything that's going on in your life. Not only do you have the authority and the power to speak to the situation, but you need to expect something to happen. You don't just speak, and not expect something to happen. If you speak to that head that hurts, or if you speak to that finger that got cut, you need to expect something to happen. It will if you expect it. I'm telling you that it will.

3. You have the power to command anything that comes against you. *Command* means a position of highest authority. You've been given that power and authority by Jesus Christ himself, the highest power! You have power and authority to speak to your mountain, whatever that mountain is. You have the power to speak to any mountain and it has to obey you when you use the name of Jesus. Praise God!

4. I want you to listen to this. *Jesus* is the name that causes every demon in hell to tremble. *Jesus* is the name that gives men the access to the glory of God. *Jesus* is the name that moves mountains. *Jesus* is the name that opens the doors to the blessings of God in your life. *Jesus* is the name that is above every name in heaven, on earth, and under the earth, according to Philippians 2:9. *Jesus* is the name that thrills the soul of the believer. There is just something about that name. Hallelujah!

I want to tell you a true story that happened to me. Back in 2001, Satan tried to choke me to death. Most Sunday mornings back then I would get up, get dressed and go to the jails to preach. I prepared two sermons, one for the men and one for the women. On this particular Sunday morning I got up to get dressed, but I wasn't feeling well. My husband left for church and I went back to bed. I laid down and dozed off a little bit. I was not totally asleep and not totally awake. As I was lying there, I felt this pressure on my throat, like a chokehold, and I couldn't breathe. Have you ever been asleep or half-asleep, and in the middle of a nightmare? But this wasn't a nightmare—it was pressure was on my throat!

I knew I had to wake up, and I kept trying to wake myself up. Then I could hear this voice saying, *Jesus. Jesus.* Yes! I realized I had to say *Jesus*, and so even though I was still about half-asleep, I whispered, "Jesus." *Jesus. Jesus.* "In the name of Jesus—" And then it was gone. You know, the name of Jesus saved my life. "That at the name of Jesus every knee should bow, of those in heaven, and of those on earth, and of those under the earth" (Philippians 2:10).

I was in shock for a long time. I got up and had a cup of coffee, and I kept thinking about what happened. I called my sister because I knew she would understand what I was saying and wouldn't think I was totally crazy! But you know, it was so real to me.

GOD, ARE YOU LISTENING?

I didn't go to the prison that morning, but I still had to minister at the prison that night. Later that day I was working on my sermon and the longer I sat there the more the devil tried to convince me that it never happened, that it was just a dream. But I'm telling you, it did happen. He did try to choke me and he's tried to kill me before.

I'm sure he's tried to wipe you out, too, even if you're not aware of it. There are so many times that an angel stepped in and saved you. Sometimes God sends his angels and you don't even know it. Praise God!

> Bless the LORD, you His angels,
> Who excel in strength, who do His word,
> Heeding the voice of His word.
> Bless the LORD, all you His hosts,
> You ministers of His, who do His pleasure.
>
> (Psalm 103:20, 21)

Do you see the power in the name of Jesus? Do you see how you are seated in authority? I want to take this one step further. Not only are we seated with Jesus in heavenly places of dominion. Not only do we have the name *Jesus* to cause every demon to tremble. Not only do we have power to command life on this earth. We have a voice!

You see, not only do your *words* carry authority for good or for bad, but your *voice* defines you. Your voice, even the tone of your voice, captures your entire persona. I want you to think about the power of your voice!

Let's look at a dear believing saint in the Bible named Elizabeth. By a miracle from God, Elizabeth was pregnant in her old age. She carried in her womb a son who would grow up to be John the Baptist. One day, Jesus' virgin mother Mary visited her cousin Elizabeth. Mary called out to Elizabeth to greet her as she entered their home. Pay attention to Mary's voice in this passage. Ask the question, who recognized Mary's voice?

And it happened, when Elizabeth heard the greeting of Mary, that the babe leaped in her womb; and Elizabeth was filled with the Holy Spirit. Then she spoke out with a loud voice and said, "Blessed are you among women, and blessed is the fruit of your womb! But why is this granted to me, that the mother of my Lord should come to me? For indeed, *as soon as the voice of your greeting sounded in my ears, the babe leaped in my womb for joy.*" (Luke 1:41–44)

Do you see it? The baby inside of Elizabeth's womb recognized Mary's voice! Imagine that! Of course, we know today through scientific proof that a baby in the womb recognizes his or her mother's voice. If the father is there and interacting with the unborn child, the baby will recognize the father's voice as well. You can see here that our voice is recognized by the unborn.

It's interesting to note how John the Baptist described himself when he was an adult. Do you see it? What did John the Baptist say about himself in this Scripture? "I am 'The voice of one crying in the wilderness: "Make straght the way of the Lord,"' as the prophet Isaiah said" (John 1:23). John described himself as "The voice of one crying in the wilderness!" John recognized the power of his voice. Even in the womb, John recognized the voice of the Lord's mother!

As if that's not enough, let's look at what happened when John the Baptist recognized and baptized Jesus in the river: "When all the people were baptized, it came to pass that Jesus also was baptized; and while He prayed, the heaven was opened. And the Holy Spirit descended in bodily form like a dove upon Him, *and a voice came from heaven which said, "You are My beloved Son; in You I am well pleased"* (Luke 3:21, 22).

You may be wondering what all this talk about our voice has to do with doing battle against that old bully, the devil. The devil likes to make a lot of noise, but he does that mostly by inhabiting or taking possession of people. The devil will use that person's voice to lie and strike fear into the hearts of people.

GOD, ARE YOU LISTENING?

What do you do when Satan is voicing his will through a loved one? It is one thing to fight Satan in everyday battles as a Christian. It is quite another to open ourselves up to witchcraft on purpose. I'd like to share with you a prayer request that was sent to me by one of my listeners:

Dear Pastor Jo,

Please pray for my friend's 21-year-old daughter. She is living at home but getting into fights with her mother and refuses to help around the house. She disappeared for a few days. I saw on social media that she consulted a medium to have her fortune read.

I feel very strongly that she is being oppressed by demonic forces. Will you please pray for her?

Charles

I prayed for this young woman, but I also anointed a small cloth and sent it to the father of the girl. I told him to place it inside her pillow. Weeks later, I received this following email from Charles, the friend of the family:

Dear Pastor Jo,

My friend placed the small cloth in his daughter's pillow, but he did not tell anyone else that he had done so. The change in his daughter was nothing short of miraculous!

She was happy, started helping with the dishes and around the house, started getting along beautifully with her mother. Out of the blue she started telling her parents how much she loved and appreciated them.

His wife even commented to him, "What has happened to our daughter?"

76

When I first heard about you sending the small anointed cloth, I thought it was strange or even silly. But just looking at my friend's daughter's comments on social media, I can see the change in her has been tremendous and incredible. A huge stronghold has been broken in this young lady's life!

Praise God! And God bless you, Pastor Jo!

Charles

I do not want to go into an entire teaching on use of handkerchiefs or prayer cloths in praying for people. I will share this Scripture with you: "Now God worked unusual miracles by the hands of Paul, so that even handkerchiefs or aprons were brought from his body to the sick, and the diseases left them and the evil spirits went out of them" (Acts 19:11, 12).

The Word of God works. You can make up excuses as to why not to use a handkerchief or cloth that is prayed over, or you can do what Paul did according to the Word of God!

Sometimes, a devil will enter into an animal as we know from the time when Jesus cast out a legion of devils and they all entered into the pigs. The pigs were so tormented that they ran over the cliff to their deaths. That's enough evidence to convict the devil of stealing, killing, and destroying!

Let's look at another occasion when Jesus cast a demon out of someone.

Now there was a man in their synagogue with an unclean spirit. And he cried out, saying, "Let us alone! What have we to do with You, Jesus of Nazareth? Did You come to destroy us? I know who You are—the Holy One of God!"

But Jesus rebuked him, saying, "*Be quiet*, and come out of him!" And when the unclean spirit had convulsed him and cried out with a loud voice, he came out of him. (Mark 1:23–25)

I want you to notice that there was *one* man with *many* voices inside of him. The man cried out, "*Let us* alone." Those voices belonged to demons. The demons spoke. They had a voice. The first thing Jesus did was say, "Be quiet and come out of him!" Jesus shut the mouth of the devils and cast all of them out in that one sentence.

Now, I don't want you to feel like this is some scary teaching. The truth is that casting out devils was a normal day for Jesus. "When evening had come, they brought to Him many who were demon-possessed. And He cast out the spirits with a word, and healed all who were sick, that it might be fulfilled which was spoken by Isaiah the prophet, saying: 'He Himself took our infirmities / And bore our sicknesses'" (Matthew 8:16).

Jesus had the authority to cast out the devil. If Jesus lives in you, then His authority rests inside of you. His voice will be heard. His healing will manifest. His provision will be seen.

Demons recognize the voice of Jesus and the voice of the Christian. We know this is true from the story in Acts 19 where a man who was not a Christian tried to cast out a demon. That demon answered him, loud and clear: "And the evil spirit answered and said, 'Jesus I know, and Paul I know; but who are you?'" (Acts 19:15).

Demons recognize the voice and the authority of Jesus and those saved by the blood of Jesus. In fact, they don't just recognize Jesus, they are scared to death of Jesus! One demon cried out with a loud voice, "What have I to do with You, Jesus, Son of the Most High God? I implore You by God that You do not torment me" (Mark 5:7). You see, we think about the devil tormenting us. The truth is that Jesus torments them! Even the name *Jesus* torments them! That's why we use the name of Jesus when we pray. Jesus has all power, authority, and dominion over the evil one. Look at our inheritance, child of God!

That you may know what is the hope of His calling, what are the riches of the glory of His inheritance in the saints, and *what is the exceeding greatness of His power toward us who believe*, according to the working of His mighty power which He worked in Christ when He raised Him from the dead and seated Him at His right hand in the heavenly places, *far above all principality and power and might and dominion, and every name that is named*, not only in this age but also in that which is to come.

And *He put all things under His feet*, and gave Him to be head over all things to the church, which is His body, the fullness of Him who fills all in all. (Ephesians 1:18–23)

We have authority, my friend, because Jesus is our head, we are His body, and He put all principalities, dominions, might, and powers under His feet. Remember Philippians 2:10 when you want to send the devil running. You say, *"The Word of God says that at the name of Jesus every knee should bow, of those in heaven, and of those on earth, and of those under the earth. Satan, you bow the knee to Jesus' name."*

As I pointed out earlier, you can choose to use your voice to speak death or life. You can use your voice to activate faith and the Word of God or you can use your voice to defeat yourself by complaining and confessing problems.

What is truly amazing is that even the people who are dead will one day hear the voice of God! That's how powerful God's voice is! Look at what Jesus said: "Most assuredly, I say to you, the hour is coming, and now is, when *the dead will hear the voice of the Son of God; and those who hear will live*" (John 5:25).

Everything that appears dead is not dead. It's just waiting to hear the voice of the Lord. It looks hopeless. It's impossible to you now, but it's not impossible to God! God wants to hear what you have to say about your problem, and God can't say it for you. He's given you the instructions. It's up to me and it's up to you to choose whether we are going to speak life to what is dead.

You and I are God's children, and he told us to take authority in this life. One day, one hour, the Son of God will cry out with His voice. In that instant, the Bible says here that those who hear Jesus will pop up out of their graves and be joined to their Creator!

Numbers 23:19 says that God is not a man, so He does not lie. He is not human, so He does not change His mind. Thank God He doesn't change His mind. Has He ever spoken and failed to act? Has He ever promised and not carried it through?

Don't you fear! Stand up to that bully. That old devil is looking for someone to devour, but he can't stand up to Jesus. Don't fear the devil! "The wicked run away even when no one is chasing them; / the right-living, however, stand their ground as boldly as lions" (Proverbs 28:1 VOICE).

The righteous are bold as a lion. In contrast, the wicked run away even when no one is pursuing them. In other words, the devil is afraid even when there is no reason to be afraid. I believe in order for you to have victory in your life that you have to be bold. I believe you have to be confident and fearless. We've already looked at 2 Timothy 1:7, that God did not give us a spirit of fear, but of power, of love, and of a sound mind. We don't have to be fearful.

I don't know a lot about lions, but I do know that lions are not afraid to take on an impossible task. They even attack animals that are larger than themselves. I understand that they are courageous in the face of opposition, and that's what we're supposed to be. We are supposed to be courageous! We are not supposed to turn tail and run in the other direction.

Let me give you a personal illustration of being bold as a lion. I remember many years ago when I was pregnant with my oldest daughter living on the military base out in New Mexico. I had two small sons at the time. My oldest son, Jeff, was only three years old, and he was outside playing in the yard. Before I knew it, he had wandered off to the neighbor's house across the street.

I went looking for him, and just as I found him, I saw the neighbor hit him in the mouth with a screen door. It's hard to believe! He was standing at the door and she just hit him in the mouth with a screen door on purpose! When I saw this woman hit my son in the mouth, something rose up on the inside of me almost like a killer instinct. Oh, yes! I started toward her and she ran inside and locked the door. Of course, somebody else saw what happened and called the military police.

Now, I don't think I would have hit the lady, but I sure wanted to! I guess the lion (or the lioness) came out in me, and I just reacted. I didn't even take into consideration that I was pregnant and that I could have been hurt. I just wanted to protect my son and I believe that's what he's talking about when he tells us to have that spirit that's as bold as a lion.

I don't think as Christians that we should start fights. However, I do believe it's okay to defend and protect our loved ones. The love of a mother will jump right over that fearful thought and be bold as a lion to rescue her cub! Just because we are called Christians doesn't mean we have the license to roll over and play dead. I think that we need to be bold as lions.

Proverbs 28:1 says that the righteous are bold as a lion. When you are established in Christ as righteous, you will manifest boldness. When you become bold as a lion, your response to the enemy's condemnations and accusations will be an unconscious thing. It will just be an automatic response. In other words, when the devil comes to you, you will respond automatically by speaking God's Word.

Jesus cast demons out of people. But when Jesus Himself was tempted by the devil those three times while he was in fasting and praying, Jesus responded by saying, "No! For it is written . . ." Jesus used Scripture as His authority when dealing with the devil. As children of God, we are the ones with the authority, not Satan.

Let me say one more thing before closing this chapter. Maybe this picture will help you. I was thinking about this one day that what I need to do is to put up a "NO TRESPASSING" sign on my body. While

I'm at it, I'll put up a "NO TRESPASSING" sign on my children, my finances, my workplace, and my house. If you do that, then you have a reminder in front of you all the time. Then you can say to the devil, "Devil, this is not your territory—you can't trespass on my body, and you can't trespass on my finances, either." He's not allowed. He really doesn't have the authority! Picture yourself putting up a "NO TRESPASSING" sign over your situation and tell him, "Devil, get out! You're trespassing."

I'm serious! Let's put up a "NO TRESPASSING" sign on you, your family, and your finances right now as we pray together:

Lord God, I come to You now in the name that is above every name, the name of Jesus. Your Word says that at the name of Jesus every knee will bow, of those in heaven, and of those on the earth, and of those under the earth. I thank You for my inheritance as a child of God, that I can know Your glory and Your power! Hallelujah! I praise You, God, seating me with You and with Jesus in heavenly places, far above all principalities, powers, might, and dominion! Jesus is the head over all and I am in Him. Praise God!

I thank You for making me Your child! I honor You and thank You for the authority that You have given me to tread over all the power of the enemy. I know that nothing shall by any means hurt me.

Devil, you be quiet and get off of me, off of my family, and off of my finances right now. You are trespassing and you have no right. In the name of Jesus, you get out of here. For at the name of Jesus, your knee must bow, right now. I declare with my voice that according to the Word of God, I am free. My family and my finances are free from all satanic influence.

Lord God, I ask You to give me courage. With Your help, I will be bold as a lion, for I have inherited Your riches, Your glory, and Your power, according to the working of Your mighty power when

PASTOR JOANNE RAMSAY

you raised Christ Jesus from the dead. Glory to God! I am seated with You in heavenly places and I am blessed, not cursed. I am so honored to rule and reign with You in heavenly places, both now in this age and in the age to come. In Jesus' name, Amen.

—⁂—

Chapter 8

The Lord's Prayer

For thine is the kingdom, and the power, and the glory, for ever. Amen.

Matthew 6:13 KJV

Jesus lived a life of prayer. He stayed connected to His Father in heaven through prayer wherever He happened to be, at different times of the day and night. I want to provide you with a short list that helps us to follow Jesus' prayer life while He walked on this earth.

When, where, and how did Jesus pray?

- As He taught crowds of people (Matthew 11:25)
- He walked up a mountain and prayed all night alone (Luke 6:12)
- In a grove of olive trees (Matthew 26:36)
- alone, up into the hills at night (Matthew 14:23)
- Before daybreak in an isolated place (Mark 1:35)
- by withdrawing alone to the wilderness (Luke 5:16)
- in the Temple, which He called His Father's house of prayer (Luke 19:46)
- with His eyes open, looking up to sky, while conversing with friends (John 17:1)

Jesus prayed often and it became obvious to His disciples that His prayer life was connected to the power of God in His ministry. One day His disciples asked him, "Lord, teach us to pray." Jesus gave a short teaching on prayer before He ever told them the Lord's Prayer. Let's hear Jesus' teaching in His words right now:

> And when you pray, you shall not be like the hypocrites. For they love to pray standing in the synagogues and on the corners of the streets, that they may be seen by men. Assuredly, I say to you, they have their reward. But you, when you pray, go into your room, and when you have shut your door, pray to your Father who is in the secret place; and your Father who sees in secret will reward you openly. And when you pray, do not use vain repetitions as the heathen do. For they think that they will be heard for their many words.
>
> Therefore do not be like them. For your Father knows the things you have need of before you ask Him. (Matthew 6:5–8)

You can see that God's Son warned against people praying loudly at church, just to be heard and noticed by others. Jesus taught that the power of prayer is found in our secret communications with God, alone in the prayer closet. When His disciples asked Him to teach them to pray, Jesus gave them this prayer model. Today we call this, "The Lord's Prayer":

> Our Father which art in heaven, Hallowed be thy name. Thy kingdom come, Thy will be done in earth, as it is in heaven. Give us this day our daily bread. And forgive us our debts, as we forgive our debtors. And lead us not into temptation, but deliver us from evil: For thine is the kingdom, and the power, and the glory, for ever. Amen. (Matthew 6:9–13 KJV)

Because Jesus gave us this prayer as His model to follow, let's take a closer look at each phrase within The Lord's Prayer.

Our Father Who Art in Heaven

We talked about the joys of becoming a parent through adoption in an earlier chapter. Just like parents today long for a child to hold and call their own, our Father in Heaven longs to be called Father. God wanted a family from the very beginning, and it delights His heart to have each one of us as His own child. In fact, when the Holy Spirit came to live inside of us, we received God's very own Spirit of adoption.

> For as many as are led by the Spirit of God, these are sons of God. For you did not receive the spirit of bondage again to fear, but you received the Spirit of adoption by whom we cry out, "Abba, Father." The Spirit Himself bears witness with our spirit that we are children of God, and if children, then heirs—heirs of God and joint heirs with Christ, if indeed we suffer with Him, that we may also be glorified together. (Romans 8:14–17)

The Father loves us! He loves to hear us call His name. Another way of saying *Abba, Father*, is to say, "Dear Daddy" or "Dear Father God." He wants us to come to Him and honor Him as our Father.

Notice that our Father is in heaven. Jesus said that in our Father's house there are many mansions and God is preparing a place for you to live there, just as new adopting parents prepare a new room for the child who is coming to live with them. They buy a bed, a dresser, clothes for that child to wear, food to eat. Our Father in heaven is preparing for His adopted children to come home!

Oh, how He loves us!

> Behold what manner of love the Father has bestowed on us, that we should be called children of God! Therefore the world does not know us, because it did not know Him. Beloved, now we are children of God; and it has not yet been revealed what we shall

be, but we know that when He is revealed, we shall be like Him, for we shall see Him as He is. (1 John 3:1, 2)

What a privilege we have, my friend, to pray, "Our Father who art in heaven"!

Hallowed Be Thy Name

The word *hallowed* means holy, consecrated; sacred; revered. The first time the word is used in the Bible is in Exodus 20:11, where it says that God blessed the seventh day and hallowed it. In the Old Testament times, before Jesus came to earth, God arranged for all that belonged to Him to be hallowed or holy, including:

- His priests, made hallowed by blood and oil Exodus 29:21).
- His tabernacle, made hallowed with oil (Exodus 40:9).
- His name, made hallowed by His people when they speak His name.

The people who lived during Jesus' lifetime knew that God's name was holy and to be feared, held sacred, respected, and honored, because they were commanded to do this in the Old Testament: "You shall not profane my holy name, but my name will be hallowed among the children of Israel" (Leviticus 22:32).

Jesus fulfilled the Old Testament command in honoring His Father's name both in his lifestyle of prayer and in the model teaching He gave us of the Lord's Prayer. Everyone who lived in Jesus' day knew the Scriptures well. They knew that Isaiah the prophet also said to hallow, dread, and respectfully fear the name of the Lord: "The LORD of hosts, Him you shall hallow; / Let Him be your fear, / And let Him be your dread" (Isaiah 8:13).

Jesus took the fear of the Lord one step further as He taught people to be careful how they handle themselves before God. He said: "And I say to you, My friends, do not be afraid of those who kill the body, and after that have no more that they can do. But I will show you whom you should fear: Fear Him who, after He has killed, has power to cast into hell; yes, I say to you, fear Him!" (Luke 12:4, 5).

So, we honor God as Father but we also honor God as the one true God, the living God, the One who has the power to adopt children and to cast the wicked into hell!

Thy Kingdom Come

My friend, when you understand the vastness of time, riches, and holiness in God's kingdom, you will be in awe that Jesus told us to pray that God brings His kingdom here to earth!

Daniel was the last prophet to talk about the kingdom of God before Christ's arrival on the earth. Daniel interpreted the dream of Nebuchadnezzar, king of Babylon. At that time, Babylon was the richest and most powerful kingdom in the world. Daniel, his friends, and his family had been captured and hauled out of Jerusalem in ropes by the armies of Babylon. God allowed King Nebuchadnezzar to experience the headiness of such power and then visited him in a dream. This dream is important because it points to yet a future time when God's kingdom will indeed come to the earth. Daniel told the king:

> And in the days of these kings *the God of heaven will set up a kingdom* which shall never be destroyed; and the kingdom shall not be left to other people; it shall break in pieces and consume all these kingdoms, and *it shall stand forever.* (Daniel 2:44)

Obviously, Daniel feared God more than he did King Neb! You can read the story how God humbled King Nebuchadnezzar by taking away his mind and clothing him with feathers like an eagle and making him eat grass in the field like an ox! True story! King Neb came out of that experience by God's mercy, and the first intelligible words out of his mouth were these:

> And at the end of the time I, Nebuchadnezzar, lifted my eyes to heaven, and my understanding returned to me; and I blessed the Most High and praised and honored Him who lives forever:
>
>> For His dominion is an everlasting dominion,
>> And His kingdom is from generation to generation.
>> All the inhabitants of the earth are reputed as nothing;
>> He does according to His will in the army of heaven
>> And among the inhabitants of the earth.
>> No one can restrain His hand
>> Or say to Him, "What have You done?"
>
> At the same time my reason returned to me, and for the glory of my kingdom, my honor and splendor returned to me. My counselors and nobles resorted to me, I was restored to my kingdom, and excellent majesty was added to me. Now I, Nebuchadnezzar, praise and extol and honor the King of heaven, all of whose works are truth, and His ways justice. And those who walk in pride He is able to put down. (Daniel 4:34–37)

Daniel had a vision of the last days that included all kinds of wild visuals. But look at the kingdom that is set up at the very end of the last days:

> I was watching in the night visions,
> And behold, One like the Son of Man,
> Coming with the clouds of heaven!
> He came to the Ancient of Days,
> And they brought Him near before Him.
> Then *to Him was given dominion and glory and a kingdom,*

That all peoples, nations, and languages should serve Him.
His dominion is an everlasting dominion,
Which shall not pass away,
And *His kingdom the one*
Which shall not be destroyed. (Daniel 7:13, 14)

Which kingdom do you want to be part of? Hallelujah! "Thy kingdom come!"

Thy Will Be Done, On Earth As It Is In Heaven

I want you to notice that two times heaven is mentioned in this relatively short prayer. Heaven is the seat of God's throne, God's judgment, His authority, and plans. Jesus only did what He saw the Father doing in heaven, as He prayed to His Father in heaven.

The Word of God says that as God's children, we have the authority to bind things and loose things on the earth. Jesus tells us all about this in Matthew 18: "Assuredly, I say to you, whatever you bind on earth will be bound in heaven, and whatever you loose on earth will be loosed in heaven. Again I say to you that if two of you agree on earth concerning anything that they ask, it will be done for them by My Father in heaven" (Matthew 18:18, 19).

What happens in heaven carries heaven's power, authority, and glory! Proper prayer always starts in heaven. The book of Matthew alone has eleven parables taught by Jesus that focus on the kingdom of Heaven!

Give Us This Day Our Daily Bread

Notice that Jesus said to pray, "Give us our daily bread," not our weekly bread, our monthly bread, or all the bread we need for the year! Jesus stressed living by faith for the day in front of us. "So don't worry about tomorrow, for tomorrow will bring its own worries. Today's trouble is enough for today" (Matthew 6:33, 34 NLT).

God is pleased when we have faith for today. He taught the children of Israel this in the Old Testament when he rained down a bread called manna from heaven. Each morning the children of Israel picked up enough bread to feed their family for one day. It was a sweet, honey-like bread that satisfied their hunger. When someone tried to pick up enough bread for two days, they woke up the next morning to find that the bread from yesterday was rotten! God did this to teach all of His people to trust Him to supply our daily bread.

Bread was a staple in the diet of the average person of the first century. After Jesus returned to heaven, His followers went from house to house every day and broke bread. "So continuing daily with one accord in the temple, and breaking bread from house to house, they ate their food with gladness and simplicity of heart" (Acts 2:46).

And Forgive Us Our Debts As We Forgive Our Debtors

If you recall, the first chapter of this book put first things first and focused on forgiveness. For that reason, I don't want to elaborate here except to add a personal testimony and to look at Matthew 18, a chapter that gives us God's solution to making things right with our human family.

> Moreover if your brother sins against you, go and tell him his fault between you and him alone. If he hears you, you have gained your brother. But if he will not hear, take with you one or two more, that 'by the mouth of two or three witnesses every word may be established.' And if he refuses to hear them, tell it to the church. But if he refuses even to hear the church, let him be to you like a heathen and a tax collector. (Matthew 18:15–17)

Peter heard this and right away he asked Jesus, "Lord, how many times do I have to forgive my brother? Up to seven times?"

Jesus answered, "No—forgive him *seventy times seven!*" (see Matthew 18:21, 22).

That sounds impossible, right? But Jesus explained that if we do not forgive someone who's trespassed against us, then we will feel tormented inside. As usual, Jesus told a story. In the story, a man who was forgiven a large sum of money, turned around and would not forgive another man who owed him a small sum of money. Let's see what happened:

Then his master, after he had called him, said to him, 'You wicked servant! I forgave you all that debt because you begged me. Should you not also have had compassion on your fellow servant, just as I had pity on you?' And his master was angry, and *delivered him to the torturers until he should pay all that was due* to him.

So My heavenly Father also will do to you if each of you, from his heart, does not forgive his brother his trespasses. (Matthew 18:32–35)

I've had to forgive people and you have, too. Jesus forgave more than any of us. He knows that if we don't release people from their sins against us, that unforgiveness will fester within our souls, and torment and poison us. "Whenever you pray, first forgive anyone you're holding a grudge against so that your Father in heaven will forgive your sins, too" (Mark 11:25 NLT).

I was preparing for a three-day revival up in the mountains of Virginia when I received an e-mail from someone whom I love dearly. I was sure that they loved me, too, so I could not believe what I was reading. It was like every word I read cut through me like a surgeon's scalpel. After reading it, I just sat there for a few minutes absorbing what I had just read and tried to understand where all this anger came from. Again, the words cut right through me.

I recalled a similar time a few years earlier when I was a new Christian and this same person cut me deeply. Back then, it took me months to forgive her and to let it go. So on this day, when I received this e-mail, I knew that I had to forgive her right away and let it go. Now that I had grown in the Lord, I recognized that it was not this person that was doing this to me, but Satan working through her. He wanted to throw me off track so I wouldn't be able to focus on the work set before me—the upcoming revival meetings.

I immediately forgave her and then I asked God to forgive her. I thanked God that even though I may not be able to do this on my own power, I could through His love that had been shed abroad in my heart by the Holy Spirit. I was amazed! Right after I forgave her, the Lord took all the hurt and pain away! I am so thankful that as I continue to grow in the Lord that walking in love becomes so much easier. Thank You, Jesus!

By the way, the revival was awesome. That was what the enemy was after all the time, but he didn't stop God's work. Praise God, the devil didn't win—God did! Hallelujah!

We are to do good to our enemy and pray for the one that is persecuting us. It's not easy, but the alternative is worse. If you can't seem to get over what someone did, then read Matthew 18:15–17 and take action. God is serious about forgiving each other!

Lead Us Not Into Temptation But Deliver Us From Evil

There are three sources of temptation:

1. The world
2. The flesh
3. The devil

We could include the fact that sometimes people lead us astray, but in the end that comes down to our flesh or their fleshly desires. Of course, the devil is always trying to work his way into our hearts, corrupting our lives and ending our relationship with God. This part of the Lord's Prayer is asking for protection from both the devil's traps and the snares of our own fleshly lusts.

If you recall, Jesus was baptized in water and in the Holy Spirit. Right after the Holy Spirit came down from heaven like a dove and filled Him, Jesus was led by the Spirit up to the mountain to be tempted by the devil!

> Then Jesus, being filled with the Holy Spirit, returned from the Jordan and was led by the Spirit into the wilderness, being tempted for forty days by the devil. And in those days He ate nothing, and afterward, when they had ended, He was hungry.
>
> And the devil said to Him, "If You are the Son of God, command this stone to become bread."
>
> But Jesus answered him, saying, "It is written, *'Man shall not live by bread alone, but by every word of God.'*" (Luke 4:1–4)

What a powerful statement! Satan did his best to cast doubt on Jesus' identity. Jesus answered that He only lives by every word of God! That's what I'm talking about! The devil kept coming back, but Jesus kept answering his temptations with the Word of God! In the end, the devil finally left him alone.

On the night before Jesus was betrayed by Judas, He asked his closest friends to come and pray with Him. He said, "Watch and pray lest you enter into temptation." The devil is always doing his best to steal, kill, and destroy us. We need to watch and pray, too.

One of the biggest temptations rampant in the body of Christ today is making money off of the sheep. Look what Paul told Timothy, his son in the Lord: "But those who desire to be rich fall into temptation and a snare, and into many foolish and harmful lusts which drown men in destruction and perdition" (1 Timothy 6:9).

The Lord lets us know in 1 Corinthians 10:13 that when temptation comes to us, He will give us a way to escape. One version says that when we are tempted to sin, God will make a safe landing place for our feet. That's a wonderful promise! Wait! There's more!

> Blessed is the man who endures temptation; for when he has been approved, he will receive the crown of life which the Lord has promised to those who love Him. Let no one say when he is tempted, "I am tempted by God"; for God cannot be tempted by evil, nor does He Himself tempt anyone. But each one is tempted when he is drawn away by his own desires and enticed. Then, when desire has conceived, it gives birth to sin; and sin, when it is full-grown, brings forth death. (James 1:12–15)

Did you see the promise in verse twelve? When God has approved us for enduring temptation, we will receive the crown of life promised to all those who love God! God loves to give rewards to His children. Temptation on earth is temporary. Heaven is forever. Let's store up our treasures in heaven!

For Thine Is the Kingdom

We are part of God's kingdom, a kingdom that cannot be shaken! Not only is God and all of His glory and power inside the kingdom of heaven, but the saints and angels are there, too. We have a great cloud of witnesses watching us from the grandstands of heaven, and one day we will step onto the shores of eternity and find out that we are part of a wonderful family and a brilliant kingdom! We are partakers in a holy dynasty and heirs of God. And our God is a consuming fire! "Therefore, since we are receiving a kingdom which cannot be shaken, let us have grace, by which we may serve God acceptably with reverence and godly fear. For our God is a consuming fire" (Hebrews 12:28).

I want you to remember that when you say the Lord's Prayer, and you come to the end to repeat the part that says, "For Thine is the kingdom," that you are in the best kingdom in the universe! Daniel said that this is what it's going to look like in the last days:

> Then the kingdom and dominion,
> And the greatness of the kingdoms under the whole heaven,
> Shall be given to the people, the saints of the Most High.
> His kingdom is an everlasting kingdom,
> And all dominions shall serve and obey Him.
>
> (Daniel 7:27)

In the end, God wins. His family wins! We win! So when we pray, "Thy kingdom come," and when we pray, "For Thine is the Kingdom," we are breathing life into the plans and purposes of God for our lives now and the future days to come! Hallelujah!

Thine Is the Power

When Jesus was on trial before the religious council, He referred to His Father and His throne as *The Power*: "Jesus said to him, 'It is as you said. Nevertheless, I say to you, hereafter you will see the Son of Man sitting *at the right hand of the Power*, and coming on the clouds of heaven'" (Matthew 26:64).

Hebrews 1:3 says that Jesus is the brightness of the glory of God and He upholds all things by the word of His power when He sat down at the right hand of God. Do you see the picture created when we talk about God's power? Little boys today are enthralled with "superheroes" and fighting men with "super-powers." Let's introduce our children to the one who holds the power of the universe in His hands!

Thine is the Glory

The subject of the glory of God is a difficult one to convey. We need God's Holy Spirit to teach this concept to us. Paul explained that glory comes on varied levels:

> There are also celestial bodies and terrestrial bodies; but the glory of the celestial is one, and the glory of the terrestrial is another. There is one glory of the sun, another glory of the moon, and another glory of the stars; for one star differs from another star in glory.
>
> So also is the resurrection of the dead. The body is sown in corruption, it is raised in incorruption. It is sown in dishonor, it is raised in glory. It is sown in weakness, it is raised in power. (1 Corinthians 15:40–43)

Moses actually saw the glory of God on Mt. Sinai. This is a fabulous picture of the glory of God. Try to picture this in your mind as you read the experience Moses and Israel had with the glory of God:

> Then it came to pass on the third day, in the morning, that there were thunderings and lightnings, and a thick cloud on the mountain; and the sound of the trumpet was very loud, so that all the people who were in the camp trembled. And Moses brought the people out of the camp to meet with God, and they stood at the foot of the mountain. Now Mount Sinai was completely in smoke, because the LORD descended upon it in fire. Its smoke ascended like the smoke of a furnace, and the whole mountain quaked greatly. And when the blast of the trumpet sounded long and became louder and louder, Moses spoke, and God answered him by voice. Then the LORD came down upon Mount Sinai, on the top of the mountain. And the

LORD called Moses to the top of the mountain, and Moses went up. (Exodus 19:16–20)

Now the glory of the LORD rested on Mount Sinai, and the cloud covered it six days. (Exodus 24:16)

This picture of the glory of God on Mt. Sinai was a foretaste or foreshadow of the glory of God promised to us today!

For you have not come to the mountain that may be touched and that burned with fire, and to blackness and darkness and tempest, and the sound of a trumpet and the voice of words, so that those who heard it begged that the word should not be spoken to them anymore. (For they could not endure what was commanded: "And if so much as a beast touches the mountain, it shall be stoned or shot with an arrow." And so terrifying was the sight that Moses said, "I am exceedingly afraid and trembling.")

But you have come to Mount Zion and to the city of the living God, the heavenly Jerusalem, to an innumerable company of angels, to the general assembly and church of the firstborn who are registered in heaven, to God the Judge of all, to the spirits of just men made perfect, to Jesus the Mediator of the new covenant, and to the blood of sprinkling that speaks better things than that of Abel.

See that you do not refuse Him who speaks. For if they did not escape who refused Him who spoke on earth, much more shall we not escape if we turn away from Him who speaks from heaven, whose voice then shook the earth; but now He has promised, saying, "Yet once more I shake not only the earth, but also heaven." Now this, "Yet once more," indicates the removal of those things that are being shaken, as of things that are made, that the things which cannot be shaken may remain.

Therefore, since *we are receiving a kingdom which cannot be shaken*, let us have grace, by which we may serve God acceptably with reverence and godly fear. For our God is a consuming fire. (Hebrews 12:18–28)

As you pray the Lord's Prayer and end it with the words, "Thine is the kingdom and the power and the glory forever," think about what you are part of as an adopted child of God! *Glory to God!*

Pray in the Name of Jesus

In one way, the Lord's Prayer is an Old Testament prayer. Jesus had not yet died on the cross and risen from the dead. For that reason, The Lord's Prayer does not conclude with the words, "In the name of Jesus."

If you research the New International Version, you will see that it says, "In the name of Jesus," nine times, and all nine verses are in the book of Acts. Also notice the POWER when we pray in the name of Jesus. Let's look at those verses now:

"And now O Lord, hear their threats, and give us, your servants, greet boldness in preaching your word. Stretch out your hand with healing power; may miraculous signs and wonders be done *through the name of your holy servant Jesus.*"

After this prayer, the meeting place shook, and they were all filled with the Holy Spirit. Then they preached the word of God with boldness. (Acts 4:29–31 NLT)

Peter replied, "Repent and be baptized, every one of you, *in the name of Jesus* Christ for the forgiveness of your sins. And you will receive the gift of the Holy Spirit. (Acts 2:38 NIV)

Then Peter said, "Silver or gold I do not have, but what I do have I give you. *In the name of Jesus* Christ of Nazareth, walk." (Acts 3:6 NIV)

By faith *in the name of Jesus*, this man whom you see and know was made strong. It is Jesus' name and the faith that comes through him that has completely healed him, as you can all see. (Acts 3:16 NIV)

Then they called them in again and commanded them not to speak or teach at all *in the name of Jesus*. (Acts 4:18 NIV)

His speech persuaded them. They called the apostles in and had them flogged. Then they ordered them not to speak *in the name of Jesus*, and let them go. (Acts 5:40)

But Barnabas took him and brought him to the apostles. He told them how Saul on his journey had seen the Lord and that the Lord had spoken to him, and how in Damascus he had preached fearlessly *in the name of Jesus*. (Acts 9:27 NIV)

So he ordered that they be baptized *in the name of Jesus* Christ. Then they asked Peter to stay with them for a few days. (Acts 10:48 NIV)

She kept this up for many days. Finally Paul became so annoyed that he turned around and said to the spirit, "*In the name of Jesus* Christ I command you to come out of her!" At that moment the spirit left her. (Acts 16:18 NIV)

GOD, ARE YOU LISTENING?

You can see that the New Testament church employed the name of Jesus for baptisms, healings, and casting out devils. What's more, the enemies of the church were afraid of the name of Jesus and ordered to Christians to stop preaching in Jesus' name. The Christians, of course, did not obey that order, because it contradicted Jesus' command to go and preach the gospel.

You will also see that four times the *New International Version* shows that Jesus said, "Ask in My name." All four statements made by Jesus were recorded in the Gospel of John. Let's look at Jesus' words on using His name:

> And I will do whatever you *ask in my name*, so that the Father may be glorified in the Son.
>
> (John 14:13 NIV)

> You did not choose me, but I chose you and appointed you so that you might go and bear fruit—fruit that will last—and so that whatever you *ask in my name* the Father will give you.
>
> (John 15:16 NIV)

> In that day you will no longer ask me anything. Very truly I tell you, my Father will give you whatever you *ask in my name*.
>
> (John 16:23 NIV)

> In that day you will *ask in my name*. I am not saying that I will ask the Father on your behalf.
>
> (John 16:26 NIV)

You may go to www.BibleGateway.com and search for the words, "in my name" and see a few more Scriptures in the New Testament where

Jesus said to use His name. Let's remember when we voice the Lord's prayer to say, "In Jesus' name we pray. Amen," it is by faith in Jesus' name that God acts on our behalf!

Our Father which art in heaven, Hallowed be thy name.

Thy kingdom come, Thy will be done in earth, as it is in heaven.

Give us this day our daily bread.

And forgive us our debts, as we forgive our debtors.

And lead us not into temptation, but deliver us from evil:

For thine is the kingdom, and the power, and the glory, forever.

In Jesus' name I pray, Amen.

Chapter 9

The Armor of God

*The Lord your God is with you, the Mighty Warrior who saves. He will
take great delight in you; in his love he will no longer rebuke you, but will
rejoice over you with singing.*

Zephaniah 3:17 NIV

When you got up this morning, you didn't put on only some of your
clothes. You didn't walk out the door without your shirt or your
shoes. You got fully dressed. When you get up in the morning, it's really
more important that you put His armor on than to put your clothes on.
Your clothes may protect you from embarrassment and from the cold,
but they can't protect you any other way.

The devil's going to put obstacles in your path, but in Jesus' strength
we can walk through them. It doesn't matter. Yes, we all sometimes feel
weak, hopeless, and afraid, and feel we can't take another step. We all face
these times when we are going through a trial. However, when you arm
yourself with God's armor you will be more than a match for Satan and
his cohorts.

In Matthew 26:53 (BSB), Jesus said, "Are you not aware that I can call
on my Father and he will at once put at my disposal more than twelve
legions of angels?" But we all know that he didn't do that. He didn't call

on them. Instead he gave his life for us. That's why we are all here today, because Jesus gave his life for us.

A legion consisted of about 6,000 at the time of Jesus. So Jesus said that he could have called 12 legions to help him, which would have been 72,000 angels.

He said in verse 54, "But how then would the Scriptures be fulfilled that say it must happen in this way?" (NIV). It had to happen that way. If it hadn't happened that way, none of us could have received Christ in our hearts.

What am I saying? I am saying that when we are fully armed in God's armor, we can take them all on! When you are fully armed in God's armor, you can take on anything and anyone because you're going to be strong in the Lord. That's where your strength is, in the Lord—and in the power of His might, not yours. You'll be able to stand.

The Lord says when you have done all you can do, stand. It's hard sometimes to stand. You feel like you've got to keep on going—keep on praying, keep on asking. But when you've done all you can do, stand. What He's saying is, "Stand and now trust Me; you've done your part, now let Me do my part. Don't interfere; just let Me do my part."

I recently ran across an email that advertised a brand of clothing that's primarily used for athletes called Under Armor. They make shirts, pants, and tennis shoes. As a matter of fact, I use some of the same brands for myself when I am working out. They call it "your go-to performance armor gear" that will wick away all the sweat to keep you cool and comfortable. They claim, "We have built these things so that they can handle anything."

As I looked at the ad for this Under Armor sporting wear, the Lord impressed upon me to teach about His armor. I want you to know that Jesus Christ is your "go-to performance gear," and with Him on your side, He is all you need. Praise His holy name!

You know, His weapons are built to handle anything and take you through any storm. Let's look at what God's Word says about the armor of the Lord in Ephesians 6:

Finally, my brethren, be strong in the Lord and in the power of His might. Put on the whole armor of God, that you may be able to stand against the wiles of the devil. For we do not wrestle against flesh and blood, but against principalities, against powers, against the rulers of the darkness of this age, against spiritual hosts of wickedness in the heavenly places. Therefore take up the whole armor of God, that you may be able to withstand in the evil day, and having done all, to stand.

Stand therefore, having girded your waist with truth, having put on the breastplate of righteousness, and having shod your feet with the preparation of the gospel of peace; above all, taking the shield of faith with which you will be able to quench all the fiery darts of the wicked one. And take the helmet of salvation, and the sword of the Spirit, which is the word of God; praying always with all prayer and supplication in the Spirit, being watchful to this end with all perseverance and supplication for all the saints—and for me, that utterance may be given to me, that I may open my mouth boldly to make known the mystery of the gospel. (Ephesians 6:10–19)

God is strong, and He wants you strong. He says take everything the Master has set out for you and put them to use. This is no afternoon athletic contest that we'll walk away from and forget about in a couple of hours. This is for keeps. God's Word shows us that our warfare is a life-or-death fight to the finish, against the devil and all his angels and all his demonic spirits and all his cohorts.

You may not be aware of this as you read this book, but we are up against far more than we can ever handle on our own. We should not even consider handling the things that the enemy is throwing at us on our own, because we are going to lose if we do. Ephesians 6 tells us how to be prepared and take up all the help we can get. We are to use every weapon God has issued so that when it's all over but the shouting, we will still be standing on our feet! Hallelujah!

Truth, righteousness, peace, faith, and salvation are more than words. They contain God's power, protection, and character. God wants us to learn how to apply them because we are going to need them throughout our whole lives.

Prayer is essential in this ongoing war. This Scripture tells us to pray hard for our brothers and sisters. Keep your eyes open. Keep each other's spirits built up, so that no one falls behind or drops out.

Maybe ministers would not drop out if they had somebody to come alongside them and encourage them, pray for them, and lift them up. You see, no one fights a war all alone. A pastor leads a church, but he's not there to do the whole work by himself. He can only do it if he has help. Everybody has to pitch in and help.

Let's consider and meditate on the scriptural meaning of each piece of the armor of God so that we can stand firm in the battles of life. Saints, we are soldiers of Christ and of spiritual warfare. God's Word says in John 1:1 that in the beginning was the Word. The Word was with God and God is the Word. So the Lord Himself is our armor.

Helmet of Salvation

Your helmet protects your head because it's perhaps the most vital part of the body, since it is the seat of all the thoughts of your mind. We can hold our head high, confident in that God our Savior will keep us, protect us, and steer our thoughts toward Him and His Word. Consider this verse: "But let us who live in the light be clearheaded, protected by the armor of faith and love, and wearing as our helmet the confidence of our salvation" (1 Thessalonians 5:8 NLT).

Sometimes thoughts come to us that did not originate with God. We all deal with that. What does God want us to do in order to combat that realm of thinking? You can find God's answer in 2 Corinthians 10:5, 6 (AMP):

We are destroying sophisticated arguments and every exalted and proud thing that sets itself up against the [true] knowledge of God, and we are taking every thought and purpose captive to the obedience of Christ, being ready to punish every act of disobedience, when your own obedience [as a church] is complete.

When our minds try to reason away faith or hope or love, this Scripture tells us that we can take those reasonings, arguments, theories, and every root of pride and cast them down and destroy them! If you find that you are struggling with a thought pattern that is not from God, speak to that thought. You tell that thought to be obedient to Jesus Christ and to his Word! Thoughts lead to actions, so we want to be sure to keep our thoughts pure and humble before God.

One of the worst torments of the mind is anxiety. We talked about this earlier, but let's visualize this helmet of salvation as we combat anxiety or worry.

Be anxious for nothing, but in everything by prayer and supplication, with thanksgiving, let your requests be made known to God; and the peace of God, which surpasses all understanding, will guard your hearts and minds through Christ Jesus.

Finally, brethren, whatever things are true, whatever things are noble, whatever things are just, whatever things are pure, whatever things are lovely, whatever things are of good report, if there is any virtue and if there is anything praiseworthy—meditate on these things. (Philippians 4:6–8)

Notice that God's Word doesn't just tell us to stop worrying; His Word tells us what thoughts we should think. If we resist the temptation to worry, we can immediately turn our attention toward thoughts that are true, noble, just, pure, lovely, and of a good report. The helmet of salvation helps to guard our thoughts from thinking evil and activates the thoughts that are godly.

Breastplate of Righteousness

The breastplate of righteousness protects and shields your heart. The heart is the seat of your emotions and your emotions need God's protection.

> My son, give attention to my words;
> Incline your ear to my sayings.
> Do not let them depart from your eyes;
> Keep them in the midst of your heart;
> For they are life to those who find them,
> And health to all their flesh.
> Keep your heart with all diligence,
> For out of it spring the issues of life.
>
> (Proverbs 4:20–23)

The Word of God is health to our flesh. When we read, believe, and declare the Word of God, His Word becomes life to us. We are healthy in body but also in all the issues of life. Also, if you know that you are righteous before God and in right standing with him, you are protected against all Satan's accusations and charges against you. What confidence we have before God: "We are made right with God by placing our faith in Jesus Christ. And this is true for everyone who believes, no matter who we are" (Romans 3:22 NLT).

Belt of Truth

Let's think about the belt of truth. Ephesians 6 says you are to stand therefore, having girded your waist with the belt of truth. Truth is the belt that holds all the other pieces of armor in place. A good way to keep this in mind is to think of your belt as the one that holds your pants up. In Christian armor, it is *integrity* that holds everything into place.

The belt of truth refers to the Scripture, as opposed to the lies of the devil who is the father of all lies.

But I want you to see that Christ is our armor. Let's look at how Isaiah described God's Son, Jesus Christ, our King:

> He will delight in obeying the Lord.
>   He will not judge by appearance
>   nor make a decision based on hearsay.
> He will give justice to the poor
>   and make fair decisions for the exploited.
> The earth will shake at the force of his word,
>   and one breath from his mouth will destroy the wicked.
> He will *wear righteousness like a belt*
>   *and truth like an undergarment.*
>
> (Isaiah 11:3–5 NLT)

When God delivered the children of Israel out of Egypt, they crossed the Red Sea. Miriam, Moses' sister, looked back across that Red Sea and saw that all of Pharaoh's horses and chariots went down in the sea, yet the people of God crossed over without a scratch on them! Look at what Miriam declared in that moment: "The Lord is a warrior; / Yahweh is his name!" (Exodus 15:3 NLT). Miriam knew the truth and she declared it in song and in dance!

Shoes of the Gospel of Peace

We put on shoes because we are going somewhere. God wants us to walk in His peace, provided by the gospel. He also wants us to walk into this world, go out into the world, and bring the Good News, announcing His peace: "How beautiful on the mountains are the feet of the messenger who brings good news, the good news of peace and salvation, the news that the God of Israel reigns!" (Isaiah 52:7 NLT).

The shoes of the gospel are part of your armor. Soldiers marching into battle must have comfortable shoes! As soldiers of Christ, we must put on gospel shoes that will allow us to march wherever our Lord leads us. God didn't give us shoes so we could retreat, but so that we can go forward and lay hold of His plan for our life and join Him in accomplishing His will for His kingdom in the earth.

Shield of Faith

Paul said above all, take the shield of faith, which you will be able to quench all the fiery darts that the wicked one sends your way. In other words, when Satan attacks you with doubts, the shield of faith turns aside that blow. But you can't turn aside that blow unless you have your armor on.

Truly, the shield of faith involves our faith in God, but it also involves God's faithfulness to us. Notice that God's faithful promises make up our armor: "He will cover you with his feathers. / He will shelter you with his wings. / His faithful promises are your armor and protection" (Psalm 91:4 NLT).

Now, if that's not a description of us wearing God's armor, I don't know what is! He covers us. He shelters us. His promises *are* our armor. His promises, His Word, *are* our protection! Glory to God!

Sword of the Spirit

Your tongue is your best weapon. God's Word is the sword and when we speak God's Word under the inspiration of the Holy Spirit, we cut off the enemy and his minions, we destroy his death camp, and we throw the devil's documents, plans, and maps of destruction out of our lives, off of our families, and out of our home!

It's all up to you. It's all up to which way you swing it. "For the word of God is alive and powerful. It is sharper than the sharpest two-edged sword, cutting between soul and spirit, between joint and marrow. It exposes our innermost thoughts and desires" (Hebrews 4:12 NLT).

Think about that. A normal sword won't do you any good. Your tongue is your best weapon—it's either going to bring victory or it's going to bring defeat. It's all up to you. It's all up to which way you swing it. The sword of the Spirit is the only weapon of offense listed in the armor of God. All the other armor and parts are defensive in nature.

God has given me a ministry to remind His children to speak the Word, so hopefully you'll understand that I want to talk about the sword of the Spirit a little more than the other pieces of armor. God called me to teach people how their words are creating and sometimes people create things with their words that they don't want. Do you know you can create chaos in your life with your words? It's true. People create sickness in their body, poverty in their finances, and confusion in their plans instead of blessings because of the words they choose to speak.

The Word of God will pierce our lives, our thoughts, our person right down to our soul, spirit, joints, marrow, thoughts, and intentions. Think about that. Speak the Word into your life, not destruction!

When you ask God for something, make your request known to Him, give it to Him, and then go on about your business. And when the enemy tries to bring something up to you, you say, "Devil, the Lord has that and I'm not going to lose one wink of sleep over that tonight. I'm not going to be fretting and anxious about that because God told me not to be anxious and fret about everything. He said but to make my prayer request known to Him. I've done it and I'm not going to lose one bit of sleep over that."

You have to talk to yourself. God did not give us any armor for our backs. Have you ever thought about that? We have no armor for our backs.

I remember Andrew Womack told a story in one of his services that may help us understand this better. When Andrew Womack was young and just starting out in his ministry, he said that people were really big into casting out demons and devils. He was going around looking for demons and devils on every doorknob, until he finally recognized that he was spending more time doing that than he was in the presence of the Lord, so he stopped it. But before he stopped, he had gone into a house with some people who said it was inhabited by spirits. They went in with the intention of casting the spirits out.

They went into the house, and there actually were demons in there. The spirits beat up on him. I know a lot of people don't believe that, but it's true. They can do that. One time I had one try to choke me to death. I do know that they can actually cause you harm.

Andrew said he ran out of the house, got in his car, and started to drive off when the Lord told him, "I didn't give you any armor for your back." He said he sat there and thought about that for a minute. He turned around and went back into the room and did battle with whatever was in that room. But when he came out, there was nothing in there.

We can't run away from fights, regardless of what kind of fights they are. We've got to stand and fight back.

How do you put on God's armor? The Lord tells us in 1 Corinthians 16:13 (BSB), "Be on the alert. Stand firm in the faith. Be men of courage. Be strong" and put your trust in His Word. And that's what He was telling Andrew. He was saying, "Be strong. Put your trust in My Word. Trust Me." We're not in this race by ourselves. He's with us, He's in us, and we never go anywhere or do anything without Him. Trust Him. God's Word never fails. Joshua 21:45 says, "Not a word failed of any good thing which the LORD had spoken to the house of Israel. It all

114

came to pass." Not just a little bit came to pass, but it all came to pass. Proverbs 30:5 (NIV) says, "Every word of God is flawless. He is a shield to those who take refuge in Him." Isaiah 40:8 says, "The grass withers, and the flowers fall, but the word of God endures forever." Hallelujah! I just love that.

In Jeremiah he says that he is active and alert to perform his word. He also says that Jesus Christ is the high priest over our confessions, over our words and he has angels standing by. He has angels standing by to hearken to this word and to *hasten* (in other words, to be in a hurry) to bring this word to pass. They hearken to it and they hasten to bring it about.

The Lord says that his word shall go forever. He sends it and it will go where he sends it. It will accomplish the thing for which he sends it. He says it will not return to him void. Do you know what that means? That means when you put in your prayer and put in your prayer request to the Lord, you're sending that word out to perform something, to take care of something.

This morning, I prayed for a friend for a particular thing. When I pray for a particular thing and ask the Lord to go before and make this thing available, I expect that word to go forth and accomplish what I sent it out to do. I'm not expecting it to come back to me void. In return, I'm expecting a good report. God said anything but a good report is an evil report.

I expect to get a good report, and I know I will if they will do as we pray. People will not always cooperate with the Word. You have no control over that. But I do know if you cooperate with the Word of God when you pray yourself or have someone else pray over you, it will accomplish what it was sent out to do. God said it in Isaiah 55:11, it will. When you are in God's armor, you are able to stand up to everything the devil throws at you.

Father, I thank You that You have provided us with an armor, that when we put it on, it will protect us from all the enemy's darts and all the wiles of the devil. I thank You, Lord, that You are our go-to-performance gear and with You on our side, Your armor is all we need. Your weapons are built to handle anything and take us through any storm. Hallelujah. According to Your word, You want us to be strong as You are strong. Help us, Lord, to put on the armor that You have supplied for us and to put it to good use so that we will be able to stand up to anything that the devil throws our way. Help us to get an understanding that we are in a life or death fight to the finish against our enemy Satan and all his demonic spirits. But praise the Lord, it's nothing we can't handle when properly armed with Your armor. And when the fight is over, we'll still be standing! Because Your word, Lord, is an indispensible weapon that no power can withstand. In the name of Jesus we pray, Amen.

CHAPTER 10

Hinderances to Our Prayers

If any of you lacks wisdom, you should ask God, who gives generously to all without finding fault, and it will be given to you. But when you ask, you must believe and not doubt, because the one who doubts is like a wave of the sea, blown and tossed by the wind. That person should not expect to receive anything from the Lord. Such a person is double-minded and unstable in all they do.

James 1:5–8 NIV

Have you ever felt discouraged in your prayer life? Maybe it feels like you can't connect with God like you used to, like your prayers stop at your ceiling and do not reach God. Maybe you lack a desire to pray and wonder what the big deal is.

Did you know that sometimes our prayers are hindered or delayed by other people who aren't being obedient to the Lord? You really need to know this. If you have a need, chances are that God is putting it on someone's heart to reach out to you or to someone close to you in order to meet that need.

People May Hinder Prayers

God answers your prayers as soon as you ask, but the Lord works through people to get the answer. God speaks to people, but not everybody that He speaks to always listens. I want you to think about that.

When you are being cursed, the enemy is using people to get to you. He is using people to make you mad, to steal from you, to harm you. The same is true with God. When God is blessing you He uses people to bring you a job promotion, friendship, or finances that you need.

We live in a spiritual world that we don't usually see with human eyes. God is Spirit. Satan is a spirit. They are both spirits. They both use people to get to you. God speaks to people to do you good and not evil. Satan tempts people to hurt, harm, steal, and destroy you.

Maybe you pray and you have a need and God speaks to somebody. He answered your prayer. He spoke to them but they didn't listen. So He goes and speaks to somebody else and they don't listen. God is faithful! He goes and speaks to another person and then another until finally someone listens to God and reaches out to meet that need.

At that point, you may hear someone say, "Well you know, I really felt like the Lord wanted me to do that for you two weeks ago." They were slow in being obedient! Just remember that people don't always listen to the Lord, so it's not God's fault. But one thing is for sure. If you ask in faith according to His Word, it will come.

God will never stop until it is done. He will never stop speaking to people and moving circumstances around until your prayer is answered. The only thing that you have to do is just keep standing and keep speaking God's Word until it comes to pass. He said in Numbers 23:19, "Has He spoken and will He not make it good?" Hallelujah!

Self-Doubt Hinders Prayers

Everything that I'm doing in my life today was just a seed at one time. There was a time when I was sitting in a small town on my couch by myself ministering at the jail and the Lord was giving me things. I wrote down what He showed me and confessed them, but they seemed about as far-fetched as it gets. Who would have ever thought that he would tell me I'm going to write books? I'm going to be on the radio and I don't even know how to record. I don't even have a recorder and I sure don't know how to write. I could have wallowed in self-doubt, but I chose to believe God.

By faith, I've written ten booklets and one book called *The Weapons of a Warrior*, and a study guide to go with it! Of course, I've written the book you hold in your hands right now. The Lord has blessed us with more than 140 stations, and we are broadcasting in London, Africa, Canada—a total of nine countries—and all over the United States. We have four radio stations in the state of Virginia and several in North Carolina—Greensboro, West Salem, Washington, and other cities. Still, I have to tell you that when God first spoke these things to me, it did not seem possible at the time. Even as I wrote them down, the enemy kept telling me, "Jo, they are just words."

I had to put the devil in his place and believe God!

Negative News Can Hinder Our Prayers

Even before he made the world it says God loved us and he chose us in Christ to be holy and without fault in His eyes. Praise God. Here's a verse that gives us good news to believe: "All praise to God the Father of our Lord Jesus Christ who has blessed us with every spiritual blessing in the heavenly realms because we are united with Christ" (Ephesians 1:3 NLT).

I think that is the kind of news that you really want to shout about! I know that every day we are confronted with messages and news of lack. We are bombarded with messages of sickness and death coming through all the news media every day on every side through the newspapers, internet, television, and radio. We get our ears and eyes pumped full every day. It is kind of like Paul said: "I am pressed on all sides." Sometimes it feels that way. Sometimes it feels like the walls are closing in on us, but even though it may feel that way, it's not reality. We can get out of that situation. God can get us out of there you know. Be careful what you allow your eyes to see and your ears to hear. We want to be influenced by God's history and God's future plans, not some fearful imagination that the news projects onto us.

Satan Tries to Hinder Us

At times, Satan is behind the hindrances that we experience. John 10:10 tells us that Satan's work is to steal, kill, and destroy. If Satan can't get us to believe and speak out words of unbelief, he presses us in and even tempts our own family members and friends to speak unbelieving and disheartening words. Chances are that we all have family members that speak negativity to us all the time and they don't really have anything positive to say. Perhaps you work with people like that. You see a name appear on your caller ID and know in your heart right now you can't handle listening to their words. Thank God for caller ID! We need a caller ID to know when the devil is about to fill our ear with negativity and shut him out, too. Cast down his temptations and thoughts, capture all your thoughts, and make them obedient to Christ (see 2 Corinthians 10:5).

Sometimes We Wander

I haven't arrived yet—not by any means. I'm still trucking right along. I may go a little bit to the left and God will bump me back over where I need to be. There's a little bit of back and forth that goes on in my life, too.

A lot of people think when they shot the missile toward the moon that they just shot that missile and whoop! It went from earth to the moon, a straight shot. But that's not true. They shot that missile and they had to correct its course every fifteen minutes. They had to do that for days to keep it on track. You know it would get over here and they would get it back over there. It didn't go in a straight line from earth, through orbit, and land on the moon! Nothing does that! It's incredible to me that they had a 500-mile landing pad to land that missile and they just about missed it. You know we all can stand to be corrected, so when you feel like you are messing up a little bit or it's not right, don't fret about it.

God's got you. He is going to nudge you right back over there and he's going to get you back on track again. Glory to God!

God makes everything work out according to his plan. Jeremiah 29:11–13 is just one of the places that he talks about his plans for us. "For I know the thoughts that I think toward you, says the LORD, thoughts of peace and not of evil, to give you a future and a hope. Then you will call upon Me and go and pray to Me, and I will listen to you. And you will seek Me and find Me, when you search for Me with all your heart."

If you look at *The Message* translation (MSG), Jeremiah 29:11 says, "I know what I'm doing." That makes me laugh! Don't you just love it? God says, "I know what I'm doing. I have it all planned out—plans to take care of you, not abandon you—plans to give you the future that you hope for." He knows that we have hopes and dreams. He knows that we have desires and He wants to give them to us.

It tells us in another place in the Bible that He didn't leave us down here like orphans. He has not abandoned us. Sometimes maybe you might feel that way, but He has not abandoned us. And it says in verse 12, "When you call on me, when you pray to me, I'll listen." I think that is awesome. And in verse 13, "When you come looking for me, you will find me." How about that? Yes, He says when you get serious about finding Me and want Me more than anything else, you are going to find Me.

Pride Hinders Prayer

When we become prideful, we hinder ourselves in so many ways. The Apostle Peter gives us a fair warning about pride:

Likewise you younger people, submit yourselves to your elders. Yes, all of you be submissive to one another, and be clothed with humility, for

"God resists the proud,
But gives grace to the humble."

Therefore humble yourselves under the mighty hand of God, that He may exalt you in due time, casting all your care upon Him, for He cares for you. (1 Peter 5:5–7)

A person who is prideful will not receive God's grace or favor. In fact, God resists the proud person. One of the only ways to keep pride in check is to consistently pray for humility. But I want you to notice that right after Peter tells us to humble ourselves, within the same sentence he writes, "Casting all your care upon Him, for He cares for you." A proud person will try to handle everything alone and resist help from God or anyone else. A humble person will realize that they are empty and lacking apart from God. A humble person will not fret and worry over every little thing because they recognize that they already prayed about that situation and they feel sure within themselves that God cares about them and He will handle it. A proud person wants to work it all out for themselves.

He does not forget the cry of the humble.

(Psalm 9:2)

Lord, You have heard the desire of the humble;
You will prepare their heart;
You will cause Your ear to hear,
To do justice to the fatherless and the oppressed,
That the man of the earth may oppress no more.

(Psalm 10:17, 18)

For You will save the humble people,
But will bring down haughty looks.

(Psalm 18:27)

Humble yourselves in the sight of the Lord, and He will lift you up. (James 4:10)

And being found in appearance as a man, He humbled Himself and became obedient to the point of death, even the death of the cross. (Philippians 2:8)

Notice in that last verse that Jesus, even though He was and is God, humbled Himself. According to this Scripture, one earmark of being a humble person is to be obedient to God. We need to check ourselves in this. Are we out to get things done one way or the other? Or are we submitting to God with a humble heart, ready to obey Him at every turn? "A man's pride will bring him low, / But a humble spirit will obtain honor" (Proverbs 29:23 NASB).

Let's approach God with a humble heart so that we will not fall into sin and God can lift us up.

Marriage Relationships Can Hinder Prayers

Another place where prayers can be hindered is when we are not tending to our relationships, especially family relationships. Look what God has to say to the husband in how he should treat his wife: "Husbands, likewise, dwell with them with understanding, giving honor to the wife, as to the weaker vessel, and as being heirs together of the grace of life, *that your prayers may not be hindered*" (1 Peter 3:7).

Our secular culture today shuns kindness and scorns honor. Our children and young adults especially are under that tidal wave at times and we need to show in words and actions how to treat one another with sweet reasonableness, understanding, and respect. It's tempting to selfishly insist on our own way, but that is not God's best. Satan may tempt us to think unkind thoughts about our spouse. Will we agree with those accusations and "put downs" or will we rise above and "dwell with them with understanding"?

GOD, ARE YOU LISTENING?

Let me ask you something: What if God treated you the way you treat your spouse? God created marriage and family to be the central foundation of His kingdom. He wants us to honor one another as the church honors Christ.

Be Doers of the Word

God's Word is like a mirror. James 1:22–23 tells us to be a doer of His Word and not merely listeners. He says, "For if anyone only listens to the Word without obeying it and being a doer of it, he is like a man who looks carefully at his own natural face in a mirror." Someone can look in the mirror, then walk away and immediately forget that there was dirt on her face or a tag is sticking out of his clothing. In other words, when we look at God's Word and see where changes need to be made, we need to make the corrections! If you have a black spot on your face, don't just walk away and forget about it. Wipe it off! You need to start doing what God's Word is showing you to do. We are to be doers of the Word of God, not just hearers or listeners.

Your spirit is not like your body. Your body can feel all these sensations. Your body can feel when you are hot. You can feel when you are cold. Your body knows when you are happy. You can feel when you are sad. And your body knows whether you are in pain or not or whether you feel good or whether you don't feel good. I know if I feel good. I know if I don't feel good. My flesh knows this.

If a person wants to be lazy, then he or she can be lazy. If you choose to be lazy, then you can't expect your pastor, or me, or anybody else to lay hands on you and keep anointing you and make everything all right! We would like to do that, but we're not magicians. We're pastors. We can only do what the Lord anoints us to do! And only He can change you, and nothing will happen but by His word. We need to make sure we are working together with the Lord and not against Him.

Our Advocate

Our greatest prayer warrior, friend, and advocate in the world today is our Lord Jesus. Jesus' blood that He shed during his torture, suffering, and crucifixion contains the power to release each of us from sin and deliver us all from the powers of hell. John tells us in 1 John 1:2 that if anyone sins, even Christians, we have an Advocate with the Father, Jesus Christ the righteous. Paul wrote to Timothy, "For there is one God and one Mediator between God and men, the Man Christ Jesus" (1 Timothy 2:5).

Of course, the Holy Spirit helps us to pray as well. Jesus told us before he died that he would not leave us here like orphans. He promised to send His Holy Spirit who would help us in every area of our lives. We see this so plainly in Paul's letter to the Roman Christians: "Likewise the Spirit also helps in our weaknesses. For we do not know what we should pray for as we ought, but the Spirit Himself makes intercession for us with groanings which cannot be uttered" (Romans 8:26).

When we sense that our prayers are being hindered, we can go directly to our advocate, Jesus Christ, and His Holy Spirit, to ask Him to intercede for us and stay close to us as attacks and negative words and thoughts assault our lives. When we are weak, we cry out! Even when we aren't sure why our prayers are being hindered, we can trust that God knows the reasons why and He will personally advocate for us in our troubling circumstances.

The Church of Jesus Prays for Us

During those dry seasons when our prayers seem hindered and won't go higher than the ceiling, God will signal another Christian to intercede for us. What's more, God may signal you and me to pray for someone else!

Are we to pray in church? Yes, sometimes. The early church lived a life of prayer, and they are our example today. In fact, Scripture shows that the first Christians were praying for various reasons and in different places:

- The first Christians had prayer meetings, "constantly united in prayer" (Acts 1:14 NLT)
- When making important decisions (Acts 1:24)
- House to house, in small groups in homes (Acts 2:42–47)
- Peter and John went to the temple at the hour of prayer (Acts 3:1)

- In the hour of trial, Christians prayed until the meeting place shook (Acts 4:23–31)
- While being martyred (Acts 7:59)
- The apostles spent most of their time teaching the Word and praying (Acts 6:4)
- They prayed for people to receive the Holy Spirit (Acts 8:15)
- Prayed before commanding a dead body to rise up (Acts 9:40)
- Peter prayed on the top of a flat roof of a house (Acts 10:9)
- People met in the home of Mary to pray for Peter while in prison (Acts 12:12)
- Leaders prayed to commission people to go preach the gospel (Acts 13:3; 14:23)
- Down on the riverbank, women gathered to pray (Acts 16:13; Acts 21:5)
- Paul and Silas prayed and sang hymns in prison, after being beaten (Acts 16:25)
- Sailors prayed on a ship in a storm at night (Acts 27:29)
- Leaders prayed for Christians, especially new believers (Romans 1:9 and numerous other Scriptures)

God wants his family to pray for one another and to show love and concern for each other. We are to be mature enough to pray for ourselves and for other people as well. God didn't just put us on this earth to get things from Him. He put us on this earth to give. God's love will compel us to speak His Word over our own lives and then speak His Word over the lives of our brothers and sisters in Christ. Each one of us goes through a time of growing up as a baby, toddler, child, teen, and young adult. But there comes a time when we are ready to aspire to being a father or mother in the Lord. You don't have to be old to be a spiritual father or mother. You just need to be mature and full of the Word of God and the love of God!

PASTOR JOANNE RAMSAY

Father, I thank You that You are still the God that performs miracles every day; and You are not the one keeping Your blessings from me.

Father, I welcome Your conviction in my life. Show me any area where I am in self-doubt or wandering away from the path You've chosen for me. I ask You to bless my spouse, my parents, my children, and my extended family members. Help me to love them and honor them as You love me. Alert me when the devil is trespassing in my life.

Lord, Your Word says that pride and disobedience are a hindrance and that You oppose the proud, but You favor the humble. So I pray today, Lord, that You will teach me to exchange my pride for humility, and give me the grace to not think more highly of myself than I ought to. Help me Jesus, to be honest in my evaluation of myself.

I pray for the grace to always humble myself, Lord, before Your mighty hand and Your mighty power. And I pray that I will not allow my pride to keep me from receiving the blessings that You have for me.

For Your Word says, Lord, that it gives You good pleasure to do good things for Your children, and that I cannot not even imagine or even ask for all the things that You have stored up for those that love You. Thank You, Jesus. Amen, Amen.

—⟋⟍—

CHAPTER 11

I Declare My Faith in Prayer!

So shall My word be that goes forth from My mouth; It shall not return to Me void, But it shall accomplish what I please, And it shall prosper in the thing for which I sent it.

Isaiah 55:11

I want my last words to you to go out with a *bang!* What better way to help you pray than to lay out declarations of God's promises from His Word that you can declare and pray out loud?

First, I want to briefly review why we declare God's Word in prayer. Remember that soil does not determine what you grow. Your heart does not determine what you grow. *You* determine what you grow. The growth going on inside of you and all around you is the result of your faith that you already spoke out loud—whether good or bad, God's Word or personal feelings.

Jesus said, "Most assuredly, I say to you, whatever you ask the Father in My name He will give you" (John 16:23). Here's one more Scripture: "Assuredly, I say to you, if you have faith and do not doubt, you will not only do what was done to the fig tree, but also if you *say* to this mountain, 'be removed and be cast into the sea,' it will be done. And whatever things you ask in prayer, believing, you will receive" (Matthew 21:21, 22).

Hallelujah! That's the Word of God. I can't express this enough. I teach this seven days a week. Speak, speak, speak, and speak. God spoke everything into creation with His words. The Bible says He upholds this world with His Word and He created us as speaking spirits. We must speak. We can't think it. *We have to speak it.* You have to open your mouth, you have to say it, and you have to speak it. The power is in your mouth. It is on your tongue. You even have the power of life and death—both—in your tongue (see Proverbs 18:21).

What we speak, we believe. And what we believe causes us to act and make decisions. "You will declare a thing, / And it will be established for you; / So light will shine on your ways" (Job 22:28).

Your tongue will guide you in life. It is your choice where your tongue is going to take you. Your tongue can take you into sickness or out of sickness. Your tongue can take you into prosperity or into poverty. And don't forget that you can praise your way out of anything, and that you will never rise above your confession.

Remember, God's Word does not return to Him void and He watches over His Word to perform it (see Isaiah 55:11 and Jeremiah 1:12). In other words, it is His job to bring it to pass and your job to release the Word into your life by *declaring, decreeing,* and *proclaiming.* The Word's power is not based on how we feel, think, or anything else, because it is living and endued with inherent power by God. What a freeing principle this is, knowing we could never ever do it "right enough." All we have to do is *speak* it, *decree* it, *announce* it, and He *performs* it.

Are you ready to decree and declare God's Word over your life right now? Let's do it!

I DECREE and DECLARE

I declare that all is well in my family, health, job, business, and finances; my confidence is in my God.

I will not worry or fret, God has good plan for my life and my family.

The Lord is my armor. I am in Him and I am able to stand up against everything the devil throws at me.

The Lord is my hiding place and my shield. No matter what happens today, I know God will see me through. I can do all things through Christ Jesus who strengthens me, and if God is for me then no one can be against me.

I put on the Lord's helmet of salvation. He protects my mind from negative thoughts and lies and schemes.

I put on the Lord's breastplate of righteousness. God's breastplate covers and shields and protects my heart.

I thank You, Lord for your belt of truth that holds all the rest of my armor together. I hold fast to my integrity as Your child.

I take up the Word of God, my shield of faith, and I have courage and armor to deflect all arrows, darts, and missiles sent against me. None of Satan's accusations will stick to me.

Lord, Your word is my sword. I take up Your sword and put on your armor. I pray in the Spirit and when I've done all I know to do; I STAND on what YOU have done. In the name of Jesus, Amen.

I declare that I rule over Satan and his house. I tread on serpents and scorpions. Nothing they try to do can harm me.

I bind all forces of evil in my life. I set free into my life all the blessings of God.

I am under God's protection. I declare Psalm 91 over my life.

I put a guard over my mouth. I refuse to say anything wrong. I speak only God's Word.

I declare that I'm in charge of my life through God's power. I am not subject to the world's troubles.

I declare I live by faith and not by sight. My Lord is a warrior and it doesn't matter what I feel like.

I am a king. I reign in this life as a king and a priest.

I take God's Word and speak it out of my mouth before it happens. I prophesy according to the measure of faith within me.

My faith comes by hearing as I listen to the Word of God.

I decree, declare, and affirm with absolute faith that I let the wisdom of God overshadow my spirit, mind, soul, and body, that I may be guided in what to say, how to say it, and whom to say it to, in Jesus' name (see Isaiah 55:11–13).

I am a vessel for the Lord. He uses me as He sees fit. He is the potter, and I am the clay.

I declare that an abundance of blessings are coming my way. Glory to God!

I declare that my body lines up to the words of my mouth. What I say is what I get. My body works perfectly, just the way that God intended it to work.

Note: According to the promise of the Word in Galatians 3:13 and Isaiah 53:5, sickness and disease are illegal in your body and are judging you falsely as still under the curse. Condemn the disease or sickness with the Word of God and command it to leave your body. Do this every time you think about it. Don't ever stop and accept the lie. *Persistence breaks down resistance.*

I am the head and not the tail. I am going over and I am not going under. God did not bring me this far to let me down or let me drown.

Note: Make a decree a promise, a word to the Father to *stop* speaking death. You are not going through, you are coming out. Decree it. Your response is not "I don't know"; your response is "God knows the plans that He has for me, I decree it."

I have victory through faith in Jesus Christ.

I do not verbalize my fears. I verbalize only my faith. It doesn't matter what trials come my way; I only speak what is a good report.

The report of the Lord is that I'm healed. I'm blessed.

I declare I have faith in God's Word and when I declare what God says, it will come to pass.

I believe when I pray over somebody else and I confess His word, it comes to pass.

Note: Please keep in mind that we do not have control over what another person might believe or say. However, if the person you pray for comes into agreement with you and stays in agreement, they will be healed.

The word is near me; it is in my mouth and in my heart. It is the word of faith that I proclaim.

God's Word is the final authority in my life. I reject all tradition that does not conform to God's Word. I do not accept anything that does not line up with God's Word.

I declare I have the same power of God that raised Christ from the dead. I have resurrection power living inside me!

My words are working to produce life, health, and prosperity.

I declare my words are increasing in power and force because I let nothing come out of my mouth except what is helpful in building up others according to their needs.

The Holy Spirit is turning up the power of my words because I speak God's Word only.

Though the outward man is decaying, my inward man is being renewed day by day.

Father, I thank You that I have a far more superior covenant than Moses had. Like Moses, my eyes are not growing dim, nor is my strength gone.

Note: I have been confessing this over my eyes for two years, ever since I was told I had macular eye degeneration. The first thing every morning, I look in the mirror and say, "Good morning, you beautiful brown eyes! Boy, do I have good news for you today! Retina, cornea, and tear ducts, I declare you are healthy, whole and healed in Jesus' name."

Father, thank You for healing my eyes. Thank You for giving me 20/15 vision (supernatural vision). I thank You that I have a far more superior covenant than Moses had, and his eyes were not dim, nor was his strength gone, and neither shall mine be. Blessed are my eyes, for they see, and my ears, for they hear.

The last two visits to my doctor I have received good reports. He said, "I don't know what you have been doing, but keep doing it."

I declare that my youth is renewed like the eagles.

Note: Ladies, I also confess this over myself on a regular basis. I say,

Father, I thank You that I am the daughter of Sarah, and as she grew old gracefully, so shall I. She was healthy enough to give birth in her nineties and even attractive enough that the king wanted her for his wife.

And then I add,

Lord, thank You that I am the seed of Abraham and Abraham's blessings are mine. Thank You, Lord, that I have your DNA.

For you men reading this book, you can confess the prayer of Moses.

I speak to parts of my body by name. I call each organ, each bone, each cell of my body healed in the name of Jesus. I call you whole in the name of Jesus.

Note: just a few days ago as I was writing this book, I woke up one morning with my wrist hurting. It was very painful and it had kept me awake. I prayed over my wrist and began to speak to every nerve, cell, muscle, and joint, and called them healed in Jesus' name. I commanded the cells, nerves, and muscles to function normal in Jesus' name. Did the pain go away immediately? No. However, I kept speaking to my wrist and thanking God for healing me. Today my wrist is pain-free. Hallelujah! Brothers and sisters, God's Word works—keep declaring it!

I declare my body lines up to the words of my mouth. What I say is what I get. My body works perfectly, just the way God intended it to work. I confess by His stripes I am healed and NO disease can stand before me.

I do not forget any of the Lord's benefits! (Psalm 103:2–5)

- *He forgives all of my iniquities*
- *He heals all my diseases*
- *He satisfies my desires with good things*
- *He redeems my life from the pit*
- *He crowns me with love and compassion*

I release Christ in me, the hope of glory.

GOD, ARE YOU LISTENING?

I live by faith, not by sight. It doesn't matter what I feel like, I am a king and priest. As a king and priest, my words are backed with divine authority.

I refuse to say anything wrong. I speak only God's Word. I am sensitive to God's voice, and I obey it quickly and quietly.

I refuse to verbalize worry. I verbalize only my faith.

It doesn't matter what trials come my way, I only speak what is a good report.

The report of the Lord is I'm healed, I'm blessed, and I have victory through faith in Jesus Christ.

The life I am now living is the result of the words I spoke in the past. So, today I am speaking good things so that later on my life will become these good words I am speaking today.

God works through my words.

I speak to my supply of finances and I declare:

1. *My greatest barriers will come crashing down and a flood of God's presence will be all around.*

2. *God's goodness is outpoured, and every door that's been shut will be shut no more. Praise the Lord! (Isaiah 22:22)*

3. *I declare God's highest and greatest blessings for my family and me.*

4. *I declare by faith that I will experience widespread increase in every area of my life.*

5. *My latter years are going to be much greater and more rewarding than my former years. Thank You, Lord, that You have saved the best for last.*

Praise Your holy name, Lord! Amen and Amen.

The word is near me. It is in my mouth and in my heart. It is the word of faith that I proclaim. I believe what I say comes to pass.

God has given me dominion. I have the power and right to govern and control.

A thousand may fall at my side, and ten thousand at my right hand, but it shall not come near me.

I refuse to say anything that would disrespect God's authority.

My words are increasing in power and force, because I let nothing come out of my mouth except what is helpful in building up others according to their needs.

I have the same power of God that was used to raise Christ from the dead. I have resurrection power within me.

I have the glorious inheritance working inside of me.

I have overcome by the words of my mouth. I have conquered the devil with words—God's words. (Revelation 12:11)

My words are working to produce life, not death. Amen.

God's Word is the final authority in my life.

My faith may be tested, but I will pass the test.

Brothers and sisters, don't stop speaking it until it comes out of your pores. Do not worry if you do not "feel" anything. The Word of God is not emotional, but spiritual.

After a few days, you will sense a change in your heart. This is where the Spirit of God always starts to work. Keep going. What is happening there is massive. This new life is better than you think, but you have to "put on" your new God-self.

Speak it to yourself over and over for twenty-one days and let God change you.

—⚭—

Spritual Warfare Handbook

PASTOR JOANNE RAMSAY

The
WEAPONS
of a **WARRIOR**

A Soldier's Handbook
for Spiritual Warfare

Do you want to win your battles?
When you are in a faith battle, you are there to invade, not retreat.

Are you prepared to stand with God at all costs?
He equips you with strength, wisdom, and discernment through His Spirit to stay strong—not only in spiritual warfare, but in daily living.

Are you tired of losing?
Let God arm you with His Word to become a victorious Christian soldier. Stand against the enemy's lies as the Lord personally trains you to wield His sword, the Word of God.

"But My righteous one will live by faith; and if he shrinks back, I will take no pleasure in him." But we are not of those who shrink back and are destroyed, but of those who have faith and preserve their souls. (Hebrews 10:38–39 BSB)

Spritual Warfare
Study Guide

This Study Guide contains the tools you need to accomplish these things you read about in *The Weapons of a Warriors Handbook*. Pastor JoAnne Ramsay outlines strategies to equip you with strength, wisdom, and discernment. This companion study will guide you into how to respond to the Lord as He trains you to wield His sword, the Word of God. This book is your spiritual boot camp training manual. Journal pages are included at the end of each chapter so you can record your personal marching orders as the Holy Spirit reveals them. Use these pages to clarify your God-given calling, and go forth with courage, conviction, and confidence!

Make sure that you don't get so absorbed and exhausted in taking care of all your day-by-day obligations that you lose track of the time and doze off, oblivious to God. The night is about over, dawn is about to break. Be up and awake to what God is doing! God is putting the finishing touches on the salvation work he began when we first believed. We can't afford to waste a minute, must not squander these precious daylight hours in frivolity and indulgence, in sleeping around and dissipation, in bickering and grabbing everything in sight. Get out of bed and get dressed! Don't loiter and linger, waiting until the very last minute. Dress yourselves in Christ, and be up and about! (Romans 13:11-4 MSG)

Speak the Word Ministries

Booklets by
Pastor JoAnne Ramsay

Receiving God's Financial Miracle

The Heart-Mouth Connection

Your Victory Is in Your Mouth

You Are What You Believe

The Power and Authority of the Believer

Putting the Devil Under Your Feet

God Wants You Well

The Prayer of Petition/Make Your Request Known to God

Taking the Limits Off of God

Angels and the Supernatural

Order Info

For autographed books and bulk order discounts,
or to schedule speaking engagements, contact:

Pastor JoAnne Ramsay
pastorjoramsay.com
855-505-2297 (toll free)

Also available from your favorite bookstore and Amazon.

Fruitbearer Publishing, LLC
302-856-6649 • FAX 302-856-7742
info@fruitbearer.com
www.fruitbearer.com
P.O. Box 777, Georgetown, DE 19947

Meet the Author

Pastor JoAnne Ramsay founded Speak the Word Ministries after receiving a visit from the Lord. He instructed her to teach His children how to fight their battles by using His Word and to make it plain and simple so even the most inexperienced Christ-follower could understand. The Lord showed her to direct His children to pray the Word of God by faith into every situation in their personal lives. Pastor JoAnne's teachings are found in her books, CDs, DVDs, pamphlets, radio shows, and YouTube videos. Visit her at pastorjoramsay.com.